THAT'S NOT THE WAY IT WORKS

A NO-NONSENSE LOOK AT THE CRAFT

AND BUSINESS OF SCREENWRITING

By Bob Saenz

THAT'S NOT THE WAY IT WORKS

ABOUT THE AUTHOR

Bob Saenz has a dozen plus produced credited films. He's optioned or sold multiple scripts and one TV pilot to production companies, producers, and studios. He does for hire rewrites, adaptations, and polishes for producers and production companies.

As an actor: Many roles in film, including *Zodiac, Jack, Woman on Top, Unleashed, Murder in the First*, and a six season recurring character on the TV series *Nash Bridges*, among many others. Voiceover on video games, documentaries, commercials.

On the Radio: in San Francisco in the late 90's as an on air disk jockey on KYCY.

Music: He was a member of the 60's rock band The BSides for 10 years.

Married for 44 years to his wife Margie, they have three children and two grandchildren.

FILMOGRAPHY

2012:	*Help for the Holidays*	(writer)
2013:	*Sweet Surrender*	(writer)
2014:	*Rescuing Madison*	(writer)
	Perfect on Paper	(writer)
2015:	*The Right Girl*	(writer)
	On the 12th Day of Christmas	(script consultant)
	Romantically Speaking	(script consultant)
2016:	*Sound of Christmas*	(writer)
2018:	*Christmas in Love*	(writer)
2019:	*Extracurricular Activities*	(writer)
2020:	*Church People*	(writer)
	The Farmer & the Belle	(writer)

"Bob's book is full of blunt-force honesty every screenwriter should digest, even if it means choking it down. It'll save them years of missteps! As *Script* magazine's "Balls of Steel" writer and Editor in Chief, I deeply appreciate Bob's candor in telling writers what we need to hear, not what people think we want to hear. If knowledge is power, then Bob has supplied us with a mighty arsenal to take over the writing world. Without reservation, I'll be enthusiastically recommending it to every writer who calls me for advice."

Jeanne Veillette Bowerman
Editor-in-Chief Script
Senior Editor Writer's Digest

"I think some people will read this book and feel disheartened and discouraged, because they haven't a clue what screenwriting is about. They have their ideas, and this shatters lofty, misguided dreams. But for those who really want to make it, who really want to do this, who are willing to put in the hard work, they'll understand they've just been given a treasure trove."

Rene Gutteridge
Head Writer @ The Skit Guys

"This is the best screenwriting book I have ever read, its way beyond in its scope for help with storytelling and format. Every chapter a gem. Bob shines light on every corner of the scriptwriting process - and how to make it work. It kinda makes me want to write a script - and after reading this book that says a lot - so much work."

Debbie Brubaker
Producer

"I LOVE this book. It is so simple to understand and easy to follow. It is a step by step guide to screenplay writing that helps you find your way to creating your script. Bob's use of illustrating what works, and why, and what doesn't work and how to fix it, is amazing. If you want to write a screenplay READ THIS BOOK."

Michael Monks
Actor, Writer, Producer

"It didn't take that many pages for me to realize I was hearing your voice. I pulled up your script *Help for the Holidays* and saw the same voice. This is good. Reading your book is like having a conversation with you. All in all, a terrific book."

Garrsion Piatte

Screenwriter

"Screenwriter Bob Saenz has carved a new benchmark in the edifice of screenwriting tomes. While other screenwriting books concern themselves with teaching you to imitate successful movies -- Saenz traps screenwriting in a net, slaps it on the examination table, and performs a vivisection on the practicalities and functions of each little detail of screenplay anatomy. This is a no-nonsense, no-bull, no-gurus nor scam artists book that pulls no punches and tells you the simple, straightforward truth you won't usually learn until you've worked in the industry long enough to know which studios serve scones on Mondays. *That's Not The Way It Works* is a must read for writers on any level who want the simple, unadorned facts about what you need to know to write scripts that sell. Want to be taken seriously as a writer? Seen as a professional? Wipe the stardust out of your eyes – read this book and get back to writing."

-Adam Skelter
Author "The Lost Art of Story"

Table of Contents

INTRODUCTION

Ok. So, there are like a zillion screenwriting books out there. Amazon has twenty pages of them. I haven't read them all. Truth? I've hardly read any of them.

Why? Because of what I haven't seen there. A no-nonsense look at the craft and business aspects of screenwriting that any new, and even some not so new, writers need to know, that cuts through all the clutter and myths and rules and formulas you read and hear about everywhere.

My intent for this book is less of a dry instructional manual and more of a conversation. A personal communication that gives insight into the realities of screenwriting, in general, and a glance at my own screenwriting journey of discovery. I think I had an advantage by knowing nothing when I started and plowing into it without finding out some people think there are rules. I wasn't distracted by trying to write my scripts to what other people say is expected. I've written this book the way I write my scripts. No rules, and in my own voice.

So how did I learn? I learned by reading scripts, a lot of them, and being on set as an actor before I was a writer. Watching scripts in use, seeing them interpreted in front of me by actors and directors. Learning from producers on set and later in production meetings. I learned by paying attention and writing and writing and writing.

I've gotten to work on set for some of the most iconic directors of any generation. I got to spend time watching, among others, Coppola, Eastwood, Scorsese, Ron Howard, David Fincher, and some of the best TV directors in the business. But, let's not kid ourselves about my acting career, such as it is. Lots of extra work. One scene parts. One line, maybe two or three. If I was lucky, two scenes instead of one. It was more of an education on set than it was a career. That didn't take away from how much fun it was to experience.

It took a while, but I finally figured out I wasn't going to have a stellar acting career. Mostly denial, I think, but I finally came to understand my limitations as an on-screen performer. Right now, I'm holding my hands about three inches apart. That would be the sum total of my range as an actor. You give me a character in there and I'm gold. Outside of that? Not so much. Yes, I had aspirations of being a successful actor at one point in my life, but after experiencing it firsthand in auditions and on set, I could see I was getting typecast.

My wonderful wife once asked, "Can't you get a part that isn't a uniformed cop or a blue-collar worker or the homeless once in a while?" The answer, of course, was, "No."

No one is going to cast me as an executive or doctor or ninja. I was once cast in a film and my character name in the credits was "Bumpkin". That tells you all you need to know.

But the more I worked, the more I became fascinated by the scripts, which I read and digested as fast as I could. How they were constructed. How they worked, and didn't work.

While working on the *Nash Bridges* TV show for six years, where I was a glorified extra 98% of the time and yes, I was a cop, right in my wheelhouse, I read all the *Nash* scripts I could get my hands on. I remember thinking, "I can do this." and yet, did nothing about it.

One day, my 10-year-old son made an offhand remark about something he heard wrong on the radio. I laughed and thought, "What a great title for a film." It gave me all kinds of ideas, so after researching and finding out about screenwriting software, I bought one and started on my very first screenplay. No books. No studying. Again, no knowledge of all the supposed rules which I obliviously broke and still do on a regular basis, though now because I know they really don't exist.

First script? Done. Took me a few weeks. Then in what can only be explained by an Act of God, that first script in its first draft form was optioned by a studio; Polygram. I know, right? Three months after I finished it.

If you ever meet me, I'll tell you the details. Suffice it to say, it was a complete utter miracle. I didn't know I was expected to rewrite it a few times before I showed it to anyone. I had no idea that it was common knowledge that it was virtually impossible to sell your first script or your first draft of a script. Silly me.

I also thought, "How easy is this?" Also, silly me.

I made some good option money, and a possible huge payday if they made it, and it was thrown into pre-production at the studio. All I knew was that I was going to be a big-time screenwriter and didn't have any problem telling everyone I knew, and some people I didn't know, about it. My ego was fully out of control. Not good. Not something I recommend.

That all came to a screeching halt when Polygram was purchased by Universal and Universal dropped all the films in Polygram's slate.

Including mine.

And, it was over. They paid me my remaining option money, gave me back my script, which is still in my unsold pile, and did a great job puncturing my rather large ego with a stadium sized hole.

It was a very humbling lesson on the screenwriting business. I went from a huge high, to a person who didn't get their calls returned in Hollywood, very quickly. Part of me is happy it happened because it allowed me some reflection time on my lunatic ego and how I could never let that happen again.

That experience, however, didn't stop me from my single-minded effort to be a produced working screenwriter. I just had no idea how long it would take or how long it takes most every successful writer. Years and years.

Later, on the *Nash Bridges* set, I heard a producer talk about how new writers really need a calling card script to break in. A script that may not get made but is so good in an unusual way that it draws attention to their skill and creativity as a writer. It was an "Aha!" moment for me.

So, I set out to do exactly that; write something to show what I could do. For my second original screenplay, I wrote a script called *Orphans* about a high school student who doesn't want to work at fast food joints as his afternoon or summer job, so he starts his own for-profit business killing parents for his classmates. It had twists and turns, very little overt violence, a lot of very dark humor and, I thought, some memorable characters. This was going to be my calling card.

When I was writing it, I had no idea that in telling that particular story the way I was, I was breaking just about every supposed screenwriting rule concerning story structure that the majestic all-knowing screenwriting gurus tell you can't be broken. Because if you do no one will read your script, let alone buy it. Of course, that's nowhere near true and never has been, and get read is exactly what *Orphans* did.

The script has a storied past. Over 18 years it was optioned eight different times by eight different producers, directors, production companies, and one studio, all who wanted to make it. I never wrote it thinking it would get produced and over those 18 years I was correct as each of these wonderful people or companies tried but never quite got it made. Exactly for the reason I wrote it. The weird controversial subversive twisty different storyline.

What it did do was open a whole lot of doors for me in LA, just like that producer on *Nash Bridges* said. After a few years of options, it finally got to a producer who liked it enough to meet with me about one of her company's projects. A Hallmark Christmas film.

Now you're thinking, *"Wait a minute, Bob, Orphans doesn't sound like a Hallmark kind of film."* And you'd be right. I've often described it as the anti-Hallmark film. But this production exec liked the writing and my writing voice.

It was my first general meeting at a production company after 12 years of trying, and afterward the production exec there gave me a script they had and asked if I'd read it and tell them what I'd do with it if I got to rewrite it. I read it, thought a lot about it, wrote down my thoughts and I told them it would have to be a radical rewrite. I gave them my weird ideas and they agreed and hired me, my first production company paying job. I rewrote it and it was a brand-new script. A new twist on the original story that left nothing unchanged. I didn't do it that way for any other reason than to make it the best story that could be told from that premise. They loved it.

It ended up being, thirteen years after I wrote my first script, my first credited, produced film.

Help for the Holidays.

The film starred Summer Glau as the cutest, funniest elf ever and amazingly enough, it was my whole script word for word on screen, something that also doesn't happen much to writers as I have grown to learn, often the hard way. It was a life changing experience for me, seeing my name in the credits at the start of a film. Something every creative dreams about.

It also kicked ratings butt, becoming the most watched cable film of 2012. Yes, it was Hallmark. No, it wasn't in theaters, and I didn't care. It was a produced film millions of people watched and, as I have also come to learn, getting any film made for any screen is a miracle. Getting a good film made is another miracle. So, it was a two-miracle film for me right out of that thirteen-year-old gate.

It also set in motion a long-term relationship with Hallmark and some of the production companies that supply them, to the tune of ten other produced films with my name as writer on them over those years. I often hear from new writers that only hacks write for Hallmark and they wouldn't be caught dead writing for cable networks like that. They couldn't be more dead wrong.

It's been a pleasure to work with, and for, Hallmark, who has quality smart creative people working there who know their customer base. It's also taught me to write within the walls of a brand and Hallmark is a very strong brand. You have to be creative while still staying within their well-established lines. That's not easy to do, as anyone who's tried to write for them finds out fast.

During that time, I also did paid assignment rewrites and writing for hire for production companies and producers. All based on *Orphans*. The script that kept on giving. Oh, I wrote more ,original spec scripts. In fact, over those thirteen years, I wrote a whole bunch of them. I optioned a bunch of them. Most of them didn't get made and that's when I found out from talking to producers that 95% of optioned scripts don't get made. It's a tough business. But some did, and between those and writing assignments where I got screen credit, I'm well past a dozen films now with my name on them as writer, with more in the wings.

Back to *Orphans* for a moment. I know I said I didn't write it to get made. And I meant that. But in 2018, another miracle occurred and low and behold *Orphans* actually got made. Now retitled *Extracurricular Activities* because producers can change your title after you sell them your script and often will. (This is your first official lesson.) It was an amazing experience for me seeing those characters come to life and Jay Lowi, the director/producer and David Wilson, producer, made it happen for me. For that I am eternally grateful.

It was released on an unsuspecting public in May of 2019 and I hope you saw it or now that I'm talking about it, will search it out streaming and see it. It's pretty darn good. Dark, twisted, not for kids, but good. Some of the rave reviews are up on the wall of my office along with the poster. Another two-miracle movie.

I've sold a few other scripts and a series pilot that haven't been made yet. And I keep writing and writing and learning and networking. My resume, even if I never sold another script, is well beyond my wildest dreams as it sits right now. Not bad for a bumpkin.

I've had the incredible fortune to learn from, work for, and work with some amazing producers and directors who have taught me more than they know, because I paid attention while they did their jobs developing the scripts I wrote or the scripts they hired me to write. They know who they are, and I cannot extend my appreciation and respect more.

I've become friends with writers who are working professionals in the industry. I've learned from them. I continue to read scripts. As many as I can without letting it get in the way of work or life. And I write. And write. And experiment with story and don't worry about those non-existent guru rules that stifle writers all around the world.

My wife has called me a "blunt instrument" because of the way I communicate sometimes. Ok, a lot of the time, but in this case, it's going to be a good thing because I won't mince words, so what I have to say about screenwriting and the business of screenwriting will be very clear.

There are a lot of statements in this book where I use the words, always and never and some that say, "This is the way it is."

Yes, I know there are exceptions. There always are. But I also know they're incredibly rare and that if a writer counts on being an exception, they're in for a hard fall. So, for every 30-year-old exception you will look up to prove me wrong, remember that you weren't that exception and that 99.9% of you won't be either. Know this book is based solely on what I have personally experienced, seen, and heard firsthand from producers, directors, working pro writers, and production and network executives I've worked with.

Screenwriting isn't a zero-sum game. If one person succeeds that doesn't mean someone else fails. There's room for anyone to succeed. Just write an amazing script. Problem is, that's not easy to do and kinda rare, honestly.

I hope what you learn here will help in creating your own amazing script and, after you write it, give you tools to market it. I want every writer to succeed. Heck, I did. That means you can, too.

CHAPTER 1

SO, YOU WANT TO BE A SCREENWRITER

Before we get into the nuts and bolts of screenwriting and marketing yourself after you write a great script, let's go on a small journey of discovery.

Story is the basis of every film. Those stories come from the screenwriters who create them. Sometimes from their own imaginations. Sometimes they're hired to write them. But after those scripts are done, screenwriters step aside so producers, directors, camera people, crew, editors, sound departments, special effects, and actors can complete the project.

Screenwriters are a part of a larger team that makes films. They're not the most important part, even though a lot of screenwriters who don't understand how films get made would like for that to be the truth.

As crucial as the screenwriter is, a script is a bunch of words that can't be used for any other purpose until all those other people put their expertise to work on it to fulfill its promise.

I have a shelf full of my unsold scripts. Unless someone makes them into a film or show, they'll stay right there. A lump on my shelf. The public doesn't have any interest in them until that happens.

You also have to know that the public hasn't got a clue what screenwriters actually do.

I go out to breakfast occasionally with some guys who aren't in the film or TV business. They're always interested in what I'm doing, because as one of my friends says, "Nobody else we know does what you do." My question back one time was, "What do you think I do?"

I was met with some interesting answers from all of them.

"You get to hang out with movie and TV stars?" Kinda. I've met some. I've worked with some. Because I work in the industry some have become good friends. But that has little to do with my job as a screenwriter.

"You write movies, so I guess, you write what they say?" Not just that. I write the whole story. I write everything they do and say.

"Doesn't the director come up with what they do?" No. I write what they do and the director films it the way he or she wants to. True, most of the time the director can change any of it, but to start with, I write the whole story.

"Wow. I thought the actors made up a lot of what they said." No. They don't. That's why there are writers. For most TV series, there's a room full of writers mapping out everything that happens on the show including everything they say.

"Ok. But like for your Christmas movie, all the magic stuff like her book and the purse that made money and her ears changing, you made all that up?" I did.

"That must be hard." You got that right. It isn't easy to do it well.

On my way home, that exchange got me thinking. What do I do? I came up with an answer I think is true and scary at the same time.

I ride a rollercoaster. That's my job. A business and creative rollercoaster that can never stop, because if it does, I'm through.

You want to be a screenwriter? Grab your ticket and come aboard. This rollercoaster goes higher and dips lower than any amusement park ride ever. It corkscrews longer and when you get to the upside-down loop it sometimes stops and leaves you hanging, making you sick on occasion. And if you're not ready for it, it can toss you out on your butt. You also have the ability to stop it at any time and walk away. Not many do, because once you get to one of those high parts you want to get there again.

New writers are anxious to hop on, in the front seat if they can, anticipating that rise, their arms thrust up high, thinking the exhilarating ride will be nothing but joy with bags of money tossed on board as the ride takes them to red carpets with cameras flashing.

Except that's not the way it works.

Reality? The ride is long and hard. It's powered by your creativity, your hard work, your determination, endless patience, skill, networking, and your ability to endure a wide array of emotions. How you handle the highs with humility, knowing they won't last, and your ability to survive the subterranean valleys will determine how you survive it.

And by your resolve to grab onto the ride and swing yourself back on after you've been thrown off.

It's a ride that's operated by people who control all of it and none of those people is you. You do have some control over the quality of the ride, however. How you conduct yourself on it. The quality of your work. How you interact with the ride supervisors as you pass them by, reaching for that golden ring they hold out.

The movie going and TV watching public? They have no idea you're even on it.

That's the truth about screenwriters and screenwriting.

It's a difficult job to get and a difficult job to keep.

I'm not trying to talk you out of it, because nobody was able to talk me out of it, but there are some other realities you need to know to be completely informed.

On average, about 80,000 scripts a year are registered with the US Copyright Office. Year in and year out. Those scripts don't disappear either. They're added to the massive pile that's already available. But let's concentrate on one year.

Eighty thousand. Remember that number.

Every year, since the birth of the digital camera made it so cheap to make films, about 15,000 or so full-length films are produced. This includes films by studios, production companies, independent filmmakers, films shot on iPhones, the one your friend shot on weekends, films your cousin made with the money your grandmother left him. Most of these are purely independent films, made for very little or no money. But they all have scripts. Somebody writes each and every one of them.

So, you have 80,000 scripts, plus the more than a million and a half written in the past twenty years and15,000 films made a year. A little daunting. But ok, right?

You think so?

Of those 15,000 produced films only about 300 or so of them get theatrical runs each year. Uh oh.

Of those that reach theaters, most of them are studio sequels, remakes, adaptations of bestselling books, comic books, films based on famous real life events, films written by established writers or established writer/directors, Films that established writers were hired to write from story ideas by producers, and bestselling graphic novel adaptations.

Where does that leave the new writer trying to break in with an original spec? A film that gets into a theater? Honestly, there's a better chance of getting hit by lightning. But, people do get hit by lightning every year. It does happen. Maybe one film or two films a year. On a good year.

And there are other outlets for film. Cable TV. Another 150 distributed there, most of them branded films. Hallmark. Lifetime. Cable channels like those, with new ones popping up all the time. Those are what I call specialty films. New writers break in there every year. You have to learn their brand and write well to it. Not easy, but with hard work, something that can be accomplished.

Then there's streaming services. Another 400 films a year or so can go directly to these services. Mostly low budget films under $5 million. Some way under $5 million. These are made by production companies, producers, and independent individuals with talent. And a great script. Maybe your script.

The math? Ok, I'll do it for you. $300 + 150 + 400 = 850$.

Eighty thousand scripts a year, 15,000 films get made (granted most of them are awful) and only about 850 films a year get seen on a public screen of some kind that generates money.

Doesn't guarantee a profit, but at least there's a chance of it. Out of the more than a couple of million scripts out there in the script galaxy.

Haven't given up yet? Good, I'm glad.

If you write an amazing script, the chances of it finding its way to people who can make it, or use it as a sample to hire you, are good. It just takes a lot of grinding effort to get your script out there, something I'll cover later.

I haven't mentioned TV because breaking into TV happens mostly after you've broken into film and you have a track record, or by working your way up as a TV writer's assistant. Those jobs are very competitive and very tough to get. That said, there is a need for scripts.

Every film or show, even a lot of the reality shows, are scripted in some way. Most are tightly scripted, meaning that the actors stick to the storyline and dialogue for the most part, and a script is used to schedule every shoot. Everything revolves around the script. That's where the film food chain comes in again.

Film is a director's medium. They call the shots. Then the producers call the shots. Some actors get to call shots. The writer calls no shots at all. None. Don't get me wrong, it's a wonderful job with a lot of wonderful benefits, but having any power isn't one of them.

I do love my job though. Being on a set and seeing your story and characters come to life is nothing short of miraculous.

If you're still reading, I'm glad you still want to do this.

If you're starting from scratch and know nothing about screenwriting, you need to find scripts online and read them. Lots of them. Read scripts from your favorite films. See what they did to make them such successful stories. Read scripts from bad films. See where they went wrong. Read scripts from other writers at your level. There are hundreds of screenwriting boards on social media where you can meet other writers.

Watch films with the script on your lap to see where they diverge or where they stuck to it verbatim. Look how script pages are formatted. Study them. Notice how each writer differs from the next. See how those writers found their own writing voice.

Those voices, each one individual to each writer, plus their abilities to create great original story, are what helped sell those stories as much as the stories themselves. I know this can be a hard concept to grasp, but screenwriting is about story and style, and succeeding at screenwriting is that combination. The mix of great story with your unique voice telling it. A voice that only comes out the more you experiment with technique and your own time honed approach to writing your script. You don't find your voice as much as develop it.

What you don't want to do is read scripts and start copying other writer's voices. Producers can spot this a mile away; a Quentin Tarantino voice, including the prerequisite "Royale with Cheese" scene, or Sorkin, or any number of masters of the craft. You aren't those screenwriters and you never will be. You need to be yourself.

One of the greatest compliments I've ever gotten on my writing was when a producer was sent a page one rewrite I did for a production company. That producer called me saying she loved the rewrite and could tell from the first page it was me who had written it by the voice and style. I wear that like a badge of honor. You should too. That's what you shoot for.

Occasionally a writer can be open, relaxed, and creative enough with their writing to find their own unique voice quickly. Sometimes it takes a dozen scripts to figure it out; to reach that comfort level with writing something as yourself and yourself only. Not trying to force it or fake it but getting to that zone where it flows from the real you. Not easy. But if it was easy, everyone could do it.

And they can't.

That said, finding your own voice is not a substitute for having to write a great story, but I think finding your own voice can make writing that great story easier.

So, my challenge to you, if you've already written a few scripts, is to look at your older scripts and see if your voice changes depending on the script or if your own unique voice as a writer can be seen in each one. You might be surprised either way, to discover you haven't found it yet or that you can see the thread of your own style as a writer developing through each script.

And don't be hard on yourself if you haven't found it yet. It takes time and knowing yourself as a writer. But know that if you try to copy the style of writers you admire, you'll probably take a lot longer finding your own.

Next time you sit down to write your next scene or script, reflect on why you think it's you and you only that can relate this story the way you want to. Then write it the way only you can. Don't write to please others. To try and write what you think others may want is a trip into the land of the futile. You can never please everyone and you can never make everyone happy, so it makes sense to be true to yourself first. This will take time.

I'll be using the word **time** a lot in these pages because it takes a lot of it to master the craft. And it is a craft. It's not just throwing words on a page and voila, it's a movie. That's not the way it works.

Most of the screenwriters I know who are successful got there because they had to write. It's in their DNA. They have stories inside they need to tell.

I never wanted to do anything in my life from the time I was ten years old but to be involved in making films. To be part of the process somehow. First as an actor, until I discovered I was a much better writer. I discovered I love storytelling, which in its purest form is what good screenwriting is. It's a tough business, as you've seen by the numbers, but, new screenwriters do break in every year.

Remember, producers don't care where great scripts come from, just that they are great.

CHAPTER 2

WHAT IS AN ORIGINAL SPEC SCRIPT?

One more important thing before we get into some of the ins and outs of what goes on the page. Let's talk about what it is you're writing when it's your own original story. Which is what you should be writing.

It's called an original spec script.

Original, meaning it's your own idea. It came from your brain.

Spec. Short for speculative. It's your own original story told in script format. It's a script you own 100%. No one hired you to write it and it's not based on anyone else's idea, book, or story.

The most important fact about original spec scripts is they are never made into the film or show the way you wrote it. They are only meant to be read.

Huh? What? Are you sure about that, Bob?

Let me repeat that so it's crystal clear: original spec scripts are written to be read. Written so the reader sees the film in their head as they read the story you're telling them. A good friend of mine calls it "Mind Theater"

You want a script that is smart, quick, and easy to read.

This is where the word "brevity", which you'll hear from me a lot, comes in. Yes, this document is meant to be read, but it's not a novel. It's not prose.

A script isn't meant to be published or sold as-is, to the public to be read. It's a document telling, in a format that only works for screenplays, a story only meant to be produced visually on some kind of screen.

It's a specialized form of writing. It's not easy to master. Personally, I think it's the hardest form of writing to do well.

A friend of mine who is an exec at a big production company told me the other day how hard it's been lately to get through a lot of the scripts she reads to find the story. It's lost in all the stuff that doesn't need to be there because the writers don't understand the form.

My best definition of an original spec script? You know all those people you see in the credits before and after a film? It's your job to do everything they don't.

You'll hear a lot of bad advice out there about what should or shouldn't be in a spec script, when only one thing should be in it. Story.

You're not writing for general audiences, yet. You're writing for a specific audience. If you write specs you hope will eventually get made this is very important. The first people you need to get through to option or sell a script are even called "readers." That's why you need a slick, fast reading script that's not bogged down with all the unnecessary stuff you've been told by some people you need.

In fact, these days the less you say the better. Again, brevity. Why is this? Because as the reader gets into the story, they get to picture the characters and action the way they want to. What helps them do that is the ease of the read. Nothing that isn't story or story driven needs to be there.

Physical descriptions of your characters? Blonde hair? Blue eyes? Brown eyes? Red nail polish? I've seen it all. Complete waste of space. No one cares. Unless it's important to the story, a plot point, it doesn't matter. If there is a physical characteristic that is a story point, then by all means get it in there. Otherwise, let the words spoken and the actions, the story, define who the character is. Let the reader picture anyone they want. It personalizes the read for them. This is a good thing.

You don't need descriptions of what anyone is wearing unless it's part of the plot. I once wrote a scene where a woman had a wedding dress on. Why? She was getting married as part of the story. In every other scene she's in? Not a word about her wardrobe. Why? It had nothing to do with story. It takes up valuable story space and it takes the reader (you guessed it) out of the story.

Other things you see in scripts you read? Or hear you need in your screenplay?

Capitalized sounds? BAM. BOOM. CRASH.

Capitalized props? CAR. BEER BOTTLE. SANDWICH.

I had one writer tell me those things need to be there for the sound and prop departments, so they know exactly what they are in the film.

I hate to tell you this, but there are no sound or prop departments in a spec script. There are no departments at all. Nobody has been hired for those positions because all the film is, right now, are words on a page. You only have departments if the script sells and goes into production, then those things go into a shooting script that a production secretary types. Not you.

By the time a sound or prop department sees the script, it's been rewritten so many times it often doesn't resemble what you wrote in the first place, a subject I'll cover in a later chapter. So, ALL those WORDS capitalized in YOUR script JUST look RIDICULOUS and yes, take the reader out of the story.

Also, don't use words the average reader will have to look up. I see these all the time. It's not about impressing someone with your extensive vocabulary. They don't care. Honest. They want plain wording so the read is quick. They have a stack of twenty scripts to get through on the weekend. You want yours to be the one that's the easiest to read. The minute they have to look up a word you've used, you've lost them.

You want an easy to read script. One that they want and need to keep reading. You clutter it up and make the read difficult and it becomes very easy for them to put down. Maybe to never pick up again. When they can get through your script in an hour because it reads well, you stand a much better chance of moving it to a different level, if the story is outstanding.

Remember; you are not writing a novel or a short story. Leaving all this other unnecessary stuff out is liberating. It actually sets you free to just concentrate on what's important.

That's all they're looking for in a script. That's what they option. That's what they buy. That's what they want to see from every screenwriter.

FORMAT

There really are very few real rules in screenwriting. Although you'll hear screenwriting pundits telling you about them, or you'll read in books about screenwriting, how there are all these rules that producers look to see if you've broken or not.

Just so you know, producers only have one rule. They don't have time for any of that other stuff while they're looking to see if your story is great or not.

That *one* rule they have? *Format.*

The way your script looks on a page.

Learning and understanding screenplay format is very easy with the advent of screenwriting software. There are quite a few software choices out there and more introduced to the marketplace all the time. Look at them all, realize that the free ones aren't really free, and invest in one that works best for you. Invest means pay for it.

If you want to use Word to save money, and I don't encourage this, you can do it. In Word: EVERYTHING MUST BE IN 12 POINT COURIER. NO EXCEPTIONS.

So, as a public service here are the margins:

1. The left side of the script is 1 ½"
   of margin. The right side of the
   script is ½" to 1" of margin. The
   top and bottom margins of your
   script is 1".
2. sluglines and Action Headings are
   spaced 1 ½" from the left side of
   the   page.

3. Dialogue is spaced 2 ½" from the
   left margin. That's 1" from the
   slugline or Scene Heading margin.

4. Character's name is 3.7" from the
   left margin.

5. Parentheticals are 3.1" from the
   left margin.

Ok, let's talk about definitions of the things you have to
have on your screenwriting pages.

Here's what is mandatory:

INT. SHERIFF'S OFFICE - NIGHT ← slugline

Gray walks out of his office over to the
Dispatcher. The
Deputy pulls off his headset. ← Action
Block

                    DEPUTY   ← Character name
Hey Sheriff. ← Dialogue

That's it. With just these things you can write a script. There's obviously a lot more to it, but this is basic formatting.

Let's go through them all separately.

SLUGLINE:

```
INT. BOB'S OFFICE - DAY
```

A slugline is the only part of the script the audience doesn't see or hear. It's location and time, where and when each scene takes place. There multiple reasons for sluglines in a script and for them to be precise. You need them for the reader to understand the continuity of your story, for budgetary reasons, and for production to schedule the shooting days of the film, if the script gets sold.

It's ALWAYS written in all CAPS. You can **BOLD** a slugline if you want. It's a personal preference. I don't bold mine, but it's ok if you want to. Nobody cares either way.

The first part of a slugline is whether it takes place inside or outside.

INT. is interior. This means INSIDE. In an office. In a house. In a car. Inside a submarine. Inside anything. Somewhere that production can control light and weather.

EXT. is exterior. This means OUTSIDE. On a street. In a park. The outside of a car.

This is important so the reader has an idea before they read the scene what they should be picturing in their mind for that particular scene. Later, it's incredibly important for scheduling.

The next part of a slugline is specifically where you've chosen the scene to take place.

BOB'S OFFICE

This is the physical place where the scene is set. This is always story driven. It can be specific; BOB'S OFFICE or a general place, like PARK or STREET, depending on what your needs are for the story you're trying to tell. Even the specific locations need to be as brief as possible in a slugline.

BOB'S MESSY OFFICE is not a slugline heading. BOB'S OFFICE is the location. If it needs to be messy as a plot point in the story, you describe that in one sentence in an action block.

You can also put other locations that exist within your main locations.

INT. BOB'S OFFICE - BATHROOM - DAY

Not that you want to see Bob in the bathroom, but he could be hiding from someone there. These subheadings are specific to your story and need to be there for the reader to fully understand where the action is actually taking place.

Next part of a slugline is the time of day you need for the scene to take place. This is here   because of the specific timeline of the story or because in your particular storyline this action needs to be in the daytime or nighttime.

I only use DAY or NIGHT because no matter if you put MORNING or DUSK or SOMETHING ELSE SPECIFIC, it will get changed by whoever rewrites it to DAY or NIGHT.

Why? Because that's how shooting a film is scheduled. Day or night. Nothing else. So why not use those to begin with? I do. You should too. It looks professional.

You can describe that it's morning or dusk in a one sentence action block

When to put a new slugline in your script is very simple. Every time you have to move the camera to a new location, it requires a new slugline.

In the case of a camera move to another location inside your main location, some writers like to use: <u>Mini-slugs</u>. They look like this.

```
INT - BOB'S OFFICE - DAY

It's empty. The door to the bathroom is
closed.
```

BATHROOM ← Mini-slug

```
Bob hides behind the door, letter opener
in his hand as a weapon.
```

Mini-Slugs can be used inside a house to go from room to room in connected scenes. I don't use them because I know each one will be changed to full sluglines eventually because each entails a camera move, but a lot of writers use them in specs for ease of read. It's purely a taste thing. No one cares in a spec as long as you use them correctly.

<u>ACTION BLOCKS</u>

You start with your slugline: `INT. BOB'S OFFICE - DAY`

Everything that isn't dialogue or connected to dialogue, like parentheticals, is an ACTION BLOCK.

```
INT. BOB'S OFFICE - DAY

Bob and Alex square off. Alex takes a
step toward Bob. Bob pulls out a blowgun
and uses it on Alex, paralyzing him. ←
This is action.
```

Action is anything that happens in your story that's not dialogue. You can also use it to minimally describe a person or a place, like the setting of the scene.

```
INT. BOB'S OFFICE - DAY

A typical writer's space.
```

If you want to describe a little more to give the reader an idea of Bob's personality, you can do that. But keep it short. And by short, I mean one sentence short if you can.

```
INT. BOB'S OFFICE - DAY

A typical writer's space, meaning it's
filled with empty coffee cups, stacks of
scribbled on yellow legal pads, half
full bourbon bottles, and empty aspirin
bottles.
```

Each action paragraph should be no more than three sentences long if you can help it. Write your three sentences and if you have to go longer, start a new paragraph.

Large blocks of words in a script are a read killer. Producers and readers see it as daunting and see you as an amateur. They will stop reading if your script is filled with long multi-sentence action blocks.

Break them up into three sentence chunks, if you need action that long in your story. This is called adding white space. A good thing for the look of your script to readers.

DIALOGUE

Everything that is said in a script by your characters is dialogue.

```
INT. BOB'S OFFICE - DAY

Bob and Alex square off. Alex takes a
step toward Bob. Bob pulls out a blowgun
and uses it on Alex, paralyzing him.
```

BOB ← this is the character
you want speaking

Take that, you meanie. ← this is dialogue.

Screenwriting software will automatically put all these things where they need to be. Your slugline, your action, the name of the character speaking, their dialogue.

Buy the software. Screenwriting is a business. You need to invest in your business if you want to make money doing this.

This is the screenwriting FORMAT. That's it. Slugline. Action block. Dialogue. 99% of what you write in a script will be these three things.

THE OTHER 1%

If you need to show VOICEOVER Dialogue, which is any dialogue said by someone *not* in the location the scene is taking place, you do this:

```
BOB (VO)
```

If you need dialogue said by someone at the scene location, but not *seen* on screen, like someone your characters don't see entering and then are surprised when they speak, you do this.

> BOB (OS)

This means the character is OFF SCREEN, but visible at the location after that dialogue. Often new writers get (VO) and (OS) mixed up. Just remember, one is present in the location (OS), one is not (VO).

INTERCUT

I get a lot of questions about this. It's used mostly in telephone conversations where you see both sides. INTERCUT keeps you from having to write multiple sluglines in a conversation where you want to show both sides.

This is a scene from my script *The Page.* In this scene the protagonist, in a restaurant, calls another lead character, in her car.

INT. GLORIA'S CAR - NIGHT

She's alone. Her cell rings. She looks at the number and answers.

> GLORIA
> You're using your own phone? Are you asking to get killed?

INT. RESTAURANT - NIGHT
(INTERCUT) ← you put this under the second location of the conversation

Peter is at the table with Caroline and her parents.

                    PETER
I'm sorry. You want me to find a
payphone? They're rarer than this
damn pager. Where are you?

                    GLORIA
You're an idiot. I'm in my car.

                    PETER
Good. How soon'll you be here?

He winks at Caroline.

                    GLORIA
What are you talking about? I'm not on
my
way there. I paged you because
there's a possible timetable change
on the target.

                    PETER
What? No. Your people just paged
and said you'd be here with the other
half of my -

He looks at Caroline, Dad, and Mom
staring at him and
listening to every word.

                    PETER (CONT'D)
- payment agreement.

                    GLORIA
Ok. You lost me.

                    PETER

Your people? The Gloria ones? Called me and said
you were on your way with it.

A moment.

>   GLORIA
Then you got a problem.

>   PETER
Why?

Caroline and her parents lean in and listen.

>   GLORIA
I was just with the "Gloria people"
and nobody paged you. I'm on my way
home, I think you've been compromised.

>   PETER
What?

It sinks in.

>   PETER (CONT'D)
Oh my God! I told them where I was.

He jumps up and looks around the
restaurant in horror. Caroline stands
and grabs Peter.

>   CAROLINE
Who is that?

Two BIG MEN enter the restaurant. Peter
moves away from the

table in fear.

The hostess grabs two menus and seats the big men across the
dining room. They pay no attention to Peter. He sighs in
relief.

> CAROLINE
> Peter, what's wrong?

> GLORIA
> Get outta there.

Peter moves back to the bar, turns his back to Caroline
still standing at the table, and speaks quietly into his cell.

> PETER
> My girlfriend and her parents are here with me.

> GLORIA
> Oh my God. Where are you?

A hand grabs Peter's shoulder. He yells and spins around.
Caroline's back.

> CAROLINE
> What the hell is going on? Tell me now.

> GLORIA
> Are you ok?

```
          PETER
(to Caroline)
Wait!
(into cell)
No,  I'm  not  ok.  I'm  at  The  Grill.
Downtown.
```

```
          GLORIA
I know it. Be there in ten. Hold
on. And get them out of there.
```

Even though the SLUGLINE says we're in the restaurant, because we (INTERCUT) with the scene in the car, it tells the reader we're in both places and it will be shot in both places. This is how you (INTERCUT) a phone call. As soon as you slugline the second location you (INTERCUT).

Yes, there is a lot of action in both places, but you continue like you can see both until the second scene/call is over.

Also, in that scene are PARENTHETICALS

```
          PETER
(to Caroline)  ← a parenthetical
Wait!
(into cell)   ← another parenthetical
No,  I'm  not  ok.  I'm  at  The  Grill.
Downtown.
```

These go, in my opinion, rarely after the character's name and before their dialogue to show action during the speaking of that dialogue. Try not to use these unless they are absolutely necessary. Readers hate them and so do I if they're overused. Don't use them to show how the line is said. That's lazy writing. Like, sarcastic or mad or happily. The story and situation and character should be enough to show whatever emotion you need to be there. If not, rethink how you write the scene.

Things like FADE IN, CUT TO, DISSOLVE TO, and FADE OUT are all pretty much not used anymore in spec scripts. They take up space you could be using to tell story and add nothing.

Camera moves, like C/U (Close Up), or ANGLE ON, or any other abbreviation for camera move or shot should be used rarely, if at all. There are ways to write action lines that tell the reader what they're seeing without using these technical terms and taking the reader out of the story.

Rather than saying:

```
C/U on a bloody knife as a hand reaches
in and picks it up.
```

You can write:

```
A bloody knife sits on the counter, a
hand reaches in and picks it up.
```

Same visual, better storytelling the second way. It doesn't take the reader out of the read to visualize a camera move. Story first.

Camera moves can be used to visually tell your story. You just shouldn't be saying "Here's a camera move" to the reader. It's another place where you have to think creatively to get what you want on screen across without jerking the reader out of the story.

SPELLING AND GRAMMAR

Spelling and grammar are part of formatting?

Of course they are. They're not story.

So, yes, you have to spell everything correctly. That means every word. Every time. You also have to get words like "your" and "you're" put in their correct places. Bad spelling means you don't care about your writing to readers. I know you do care. So, spell "your" words correctly while "you're" writing.

Grammar is a whole other thing. Yes, in your action sequences grammar counts to a large extent. Correct grammar will make your action lines easier to understand and not take the reader out of the story wondering if you got past third grade or not.

But contractions are your friend, use them. You can also use incomplete sentences in your action lines if you want, for effect. You can even use one-word sentences, again, for effect.

Brevity. In further chapters when I talk about building action sequences and writing dialogue, I will elaborate on this.

The upshot, you need to write like you passed English class and retained what you learned. Anything less will result in unreadable scripts. No reader or producer is going to slog through your bad spelling and grammar even if you have a great story in there.

And now for the exception: You can use bad grammar in dialogue. Human beings don't speak with proper grammar.

Bad grammar and spelling are not things to sluff off thinking that someone else will clean up your mistakes.

This is something you have to learn to do yourself. There are no editors in screenwriting. Yes, some enterprising people have set up businesses to edit scripts for spelling and grammar, but when you get to a producer with your work and can't do it yourself, and believe me they'll figure it out fast, you'll be fired and never rehired.

Again, for emphasis. Producers and production companies and directors don't use editors, they just hire another screenwriter (that isn't you) to rewrite your script if you can't do these things for yourself.

Never ever have someone else edit your script, then pass the script off as if you did all the work, it will catch up with you and not in a good way. You have been warned.

SCREENPLAYS ARE ACTIVE, NOT PASSIVE

This is very important in formatting your script. You write what happens, not what is happening. It's active. Meaning, you limit words ending with "-ing" to when they are active words.

Example:

```
INT. OFFICE - DAY
```

Bob walks into the room. ← This is active. He walks.

Versus:

```
INT. OFFICE - DAY
```

Bob is walking into the room. ← this is wrong.

Every action line you write is active. It happens. It's not happening.

So, people walk, run, dance, sit,You get the idea.

They aren't walking, running, dancing, or sitting.

Bob is sitting in the chair. ← wrong

Bob sits in the chair. ← correct

All -ing words are not bad. You just have to be careful with their usage.

This isn't a rule. This is standard formatting of scripts, just like sluglines are standard formatting. It makes scripts read like they happen in front of the reader, making it easier for them to see it as a film in their head.

REAL TIME

Most of the scripts I read, to be polite, and we should always try to be polite, are,lacking. Some in big ways. Some in huge ways. It's hard to tell someone their subject matter, their premise, won't sell tickets or cause someone to hit the button on their remote to watch, ever. Or to tell someone their script has enough plot holes in it to fill the Albert Hall, a Beatles reference, if you don't know it. Nobody wants to hear these things, but better to hear them now and be able to learn them so you avoid making the same mistakes over and over.

But c'mon, even if your story is lacking, you shouldn't be making glaring technical format errors. There is no excuse in the world for that. Some of these errors are so bad it makes me think, a lot of the time, that the writer never really reads what they wrote. They throw words on a page and never carefully look at them again. Some of these technical format errors are pet peeves of mine.

At the top of my peeve list is the subject of REAL TIME.

Ninety-nine percent of movie and TV stories take place in real time. Unless you use some story device to suspend real time, and there have been films that have done this successfully, what you write in a scene happens in the time you describe. You are telling the reader; this is what you're going to see take place on screen in my story.

Your words commit you to it and commit your story to it.

Real Time means there's a clock running on every scene. That clock times how long that scene is onscreen. A clock that is counting the length of your film, scene by scene. All the scenes need to add up to less than two hours, and in a perfect world, closer to an hour and a half, for a film. Same for your hour-long pilot or half hour comedy show.

You need to take into account that clock as you write any action in any scene. This is something novelists never have to think about. It's exclusive to screenwriting which is why so many new writers don't grasp it right away.

Better to start thinking about it now, as you're maybe starting out, than to send a script out with this kind of glaring technical error. And if you have a few scripts under your belt, time to go back and look at them carefully to see if this may have contributed to some of the passes you've gotten on your work.

Let me give you an example of correct real time:

EXT. OLDER OFFICE BUILDING - DAY

Bobette   and   Bob   emerge   from   the
building. Bobette holds
Bob by the ear and pulls him.

                    BOB
Ok. Ok. I said I'd go. Ok?

That's the whole scene; 1/8 of a page. Let's break it down: Bobette and Bob emerge from an office building door; Bobette firmly gripping Bob by the ear; pulls him along; Bob says one line of dialogue.

If you saw this in real life on the street it would take, what, maybe 15 - 20 seconds at the longest to take place. That 15 – 20 seconds it took, is real time, just like it's described. The clock in real life ran exactly as long as it should take to accomplish this action, this scene, on screen.

When you describe something in your scene, your job is to account for that clock by the way you word your script. Those words will dictate how long it will take for your characters to do whatever it is you're describing. You're telling the reader that's how long on screen, timewise, your scene will be. You're not telling them how long your scene *should* be, but how long it *will* be.

How long in seconds, minutes, or in the case of really bad writing; hours, that scene takes of screen time. Hours? Is that possible for one scene? You bet. If they write it that way. It's not what the writer intends, but that's the way it reads.

Here's an example of something like I've read in multiple scripts in the past, all making the mistake of not thinking about that clock that's running from start to finish on each scene.

```
INT. RESTAURANT - DINING AREA -- DAY

Bob and Bobette take their seats at the
table. Bob reaches
out his hand and takes hers in it.

          BOB
Wanna do the salad bar? I know
you're on a diet and I'm trying to
be more sensitive.
```

Bobette pulls her hand away.

            BOBETTE
You trying to tell me I'm fat? I
wore my skinny jeans.

            BOB
No. Of course not. I'm uh…hungry
for a salad. That's all. C'mon.

They stand and walk to the salad bar and
make their salads,
returning to their table, sitting down
and eating.

They finish their salads.

            BOBETTE
You know, that really was a good
salad. Thank you for suggesting it.

Bob smiles triumphantly.

Let's break this scene down. An unfeeling jerk tells his girlfriend she's fat. She reacts, he sluffs it off. I just timed it on the clock in my office. Ten seconds. Real time.

Then they get up, walk to the salad bar, and make their salads. I don't know about you, but I don't want to take four or five minutes of my time to watch these people walk to a salad bar, make a salad, carefully choosing each ingredient, and then take it back to their table and, to top it off, eat it all, with no dialogue.

That's exactly what's described in the action lines. The words the writer chose. Those words make it look like the writer wants the audience to sit in silence watching these characters build a salad then take it back to the table and stuff their faces. Oh, the suspense of what dressing they choose. Will they like it or not? Is that arugula in her teeth? Was it as good as it looked?

Taking into account the running clock, this scene, as written, takes about 20 to 30 minutes of screen time. In an hour and half film. Doesn't leave a lot of time for the rest of the story.

Ok, we know that's not what the writer wanted or meant, unless they're insane or Andy Warhol, but that's exactly what's described in the scene. Exactly, in real time.

I know you're thinking, oh c'mon, the reader understands thast not what the writer intended. They do. They also see it through the lens of "This writer doesn't know how to write a script."

It reflects on you as a writer. It shows haphazard, thoughtless writing. No care in choosing the correct words you need to write a coherent scene that happens in the time it needs to. They will put your script down if you do this. This is bad writing. There is no excuse for doing something like this if you care about your words.

Here's another example, because I need to cement this with you, it's that important. I once got a script where an action line read something like this:

```
EXT. ROADWAY - DAY

Bob stands by the side of the road and
hitchhikes for an hour, watching cars
```

pass him by, before a white Limousine pulls up.

I laughed. I thought, "Man, that's one long scene." Yeah, as written, even though I'm sure it's not what the writer meant, this scene uses an hour of precious screen time with absolutely nothing going on.

Action lines are literal. One hour of screen time in this writer's story is gone. Poof.

If you think this isn't a huge error, you'd be wrong. That line alone, if it's early in a script, could be enough to have a reader put your script down, rejecting it.

Yes, the intent of the scene is to show the passage of time, but the writer chose the laziest, most unthinking way. It's your job to look at every word in every scene to make sure this doesn't happen. Again, it's work. It's attention to detail. It's your job if you want to do this for a living. So, how do you write the above and make it work in real time? Glad you asked. Couple of ways.

EXT. ROADSIDE - DAY

Bob stands, watching cars whiz by, thumb out, waiting for a
ride.

MONTAGE: Quick cuts

Bob dances around as he sticks his thumb out.

Bob moves his thumb from place to place. Over his head,

under his arm, under his leg as cars quickly pass.

Bob sits on the side of the road, thumb out.

Bob shakes his fist as cars go by, not stopping.

Bob walks down the road, thumb halfway out, back to the cars as they pass.

EXT. ROADSIDE - DAY

A large white Limo drives past Bob and pulls over. The back door opens. Bob runs to the open door.

OR

TIME LAPSE.

Bob stands, sits, moves as cars streak by in fast motion.

EXT. ROADSIDE - DAY

A large white Limo drives past Bob and pulls over. The back door opens. Bob runs to the open door.

Either works. I like the first one, but both will work to show what you want and both look like you know what you're doing.

Good readers, pro readers, producers, notice this. Understand, they know that's not what the writer meant. They recognize that it's a technical error. But it is what the writer wrote. It's right there on the page. They know if you're not on the ball enough to see these things, to be a good enough writer to pay attention to your wording, it's gonna be a long read. It colors the way they look at your script from that point on. If they decide to read any further. They may not.

Look back at your old scripts. I hope you don't find these things. You might though. And from this day forward, think in real time. How much time is what I am describing going to take on screen? The clock is running.

It's such a simple thing.

TITLE PAGE

You need a title page. For that, you need a title. My advice for titles? Short. Sweet. Has something to do with your story. Don't fall in love with them. Don't try and be too clever. And know this, they get changed all the time.

My film *Extracurricular Activities* was once titled *Orphans*. It got changed twice by producers along the way to production, from *Orphans* to *Extracurricular Activities* to *Delinquents* and back to *Extracurricular Activities*. It happens. They get to do that. You can't do anything about it.

So, make up something that's one to four words if you can. Snappy. Memorable.

The screenwriting software programs all have title page templates. You put the title in the upper middle of the page with your name under it.

```
ORPHANS

By Bob Saenz
```

That's it; title and your name alone or with a writing partner, if you have one. If you have a writing partner. It looks like this:

```
TITLE

By Bob Bobette & Bobette Bob
```

You use "&" and not "and". I'll explain this later when I talk about Credits. Just trust me and use the "&".

What you don't put on the title page under your name?

No Copyright Number. No WGA reg number, if you choose to get one. No nothing.

Why? First, because producers give you credit for being smart enough to copyright your script. So, it's not a requirement. No need for it. Secondly, those numbers can be traced to the year they were assigned, so producers can tell how old your script is. This, you do not want them to know. You always want people reading your script for the first time to think that it's new. Why? Nobody wants to read an old script. Producers want to think they are reading your latest opus. So, you treat your script as new every time you send it out. We know that scripts can sit for years before they get made, so why advertise it. Leave the numbers off.

In the bottom left corner of the title page you put your contact info.

```
BobBobette@email.com

(555)555-5555
```

Your email and cell number. That's it. Never your home address. Never.

Scripts, especially in PDF format, can end up on the internet and in the hands of all kinds of people and you don't want your address on there. Some people just put their email, leaving their cell number off. This might not be a bad thing.

Title pages are very simple things.

The next question I get usually is: Can I put an image on my title page?

The gurus will say "NO!!!!!! Producers will see this image on your title page and cry or scream as they toss your script into boiling oil." The gurus, again, would be wrong.

If you have an appropriate image to put on your title page that is tasteful, that works with your title and story, of course you can use one. I've seen a lot of them that were great, including on scripts that got sold and produced. Don't go overboard. Don't spend a lot of time on it because it's about your story, not how cool your title page is.

Remember: Screenwriting software does a lot of the formatting for you. It puts things like sluglines, action blocks, and dialogue where they should be on the page and helps you build your title page. They remember your characters. They remember your locations. They put everything where it's supposed to go.

But there are things it doesn't do:

Screenwriting software does not fix your spelling or grammar or write your script as an active document or in real time, or most of all, write your story for you. It's a tool to relieve you of having to think about putting these things where they need to go on the page. That's it.

You still have to do all the heavy lifting.

CHAPTER 3

CHOOSING YOUR STORY/PREMISE

I know this seems like something you don't need help with. You want to be a screenwriter, so deciding on the story you want to tell should be something that's personal and easy. And it is, if you don't care whether other people want to read your script or not.

The problem? Most story ideas beginning screenwriters come up with are terrible. There's no audience for them or the audience for them is tired of them or they are ideas that already play on TV series reruns 24 hours a day.

I've read scripts about car repair, painting a mural, scrapbooking, one that was so boring and bad as the writer explained in great detail every aspect of scrapbooking, FBI agents revenging their dead families, a particular favorite, retread zombie scripts, and all kinds of subject matter that no matter how you write it, doesn't lend itself to a viable or producible, compelling script.

One of the worst pieces of advice I hear given to screenwriters is "Write only what you know." Well, this is what leads to scripts about scrapbooking. Yes, you as a writer do need to draw on your experiences to write, but most great writers pick premises that interest them, and are compelling or high concept, and worthy of a film that can attract an audience and then they go out and work to learn all they can about the subject matter. They don't write what they know, they know what they write.

BUCKET LISTS & LIVING A LIFE

Can you make the film industry the foremost thing in your life and be a successful screenwriter?

In my opinion, no.

Every writer draws on something of their own experiences when they write. It doesn't matter what the story or subject matter is, every writer puts some of themselves in there. They're personal. When you're out living your real life, you can find the ideas that end up being your stories. It's where you find characters and dialogue.

If you focus your life only on screenwriting and everything film or TV, you lose out on the life experiences that make writing real. You don't have personal experiences to draw on.

Go out and live a full life as you write your scripts. Have interests outside of writing. Have those things to draw on. You'll never know when something you do outside of just writing and this industry will spur you on to your greatest work.

To that end, I have a Bucket List. I've had it since I was thirteen years old. On it are all kinds of things I wanted, and still want to do, to experience. Things like climbing a mountain, whitewater rafting the Colorado River, going to

Europe, Asia, playing in a rock and roll band in front of a big crowd, acting in a movie, going into space, flying seaplanes in Alaska, going to a Broadway show, being in a Broadway show, skiing in Colorado, sky diving, playing golf in Scotland; the list goes on and on. I've done a whole lot of them. Not all. Haven't gone to space yet, but there's still time. What did I learn?

More than I ever could looking this stuff up online, I can tell you that. The visceral feeling of experiencing these things will be part of me forever. Physical and emotional memories that I use all the time in my writing.

Don't just sit and write. Go out and live your life. This will help you as much as good research, which you also need to do to be a good writer.

RESEARCH

Again, writers should be drawing on their personal experiences for sure, because what you've seen and heard for real can be used as real in your writing, even if you have to enhance it or use it out of its original context. That's writing. That's creativity.

But writers, most writers, come up with ideas for scripts all the time on subjects they know nothing about and what separates the good writers from the pack is what they do about it.

Good writers research. Real research. They don't just do a cursory internet search. They get out there in the real world and find the information to bring authenticity to whatever they're writing about. They ground their stories in the reality of the subject matter.

I read a script once that mostly took place in a hospital. To say this might have been the worst script I have ever read is giving it some credit. The paper it was printed on threw up a little knowing what was written there. Nonetheless, the hospital scenes were extra astounding due to the fact that the writer got everything about them 100% wrong.

Where do I start? Ok, a nurse who is an integral part of the plot is only a registered nurse working at the hospital because it's part of her community service for being arrested for prostitution. I know, right? I'm not kidding. No nursing school. No nursing license. Community service for being caught hooking. This would happen in real life…never.

If that alone wasn't bad enough, the protagonist uses vacant operating rooms in the hospital to do complicated illegal operations on someone as part of a revenge plan, without anyone at the hospital knowing or finding out. They then use a spare hospital room for this same person while they recover, keeping it a secret from everyone who works there.

I asked him, "Where is this hospital? On Mars? A different dimension?" I then asked him if he had done one second of research on how hospitals really work. I knew the answer was "No.", but I had to ask. I then told him that none if this would happen in any hospital in this country, ever.

His answer was, "But it's a movie. It's not real." It was then that I thanked him for letting me read his opus and made a quick getaway.

Most all scripts are fictional and most are set in the real world and thus, need to be grounded in that world. If you're going to be writing a film about the Secret Service, you need to find out how they operate. If you're setting a film in a hospital or crime lab or anywhere else real, you need to learn the reality of those places, so your script is steeped in that reality. You make stuff up for your story from that knowledge.

If your characters are doctors or cops or lawyers or scientists or any profession that requires a specific knowledge or ability, it's your job to obtain enough of that knowledge to write intelligently about it. And, not surprisingly, you'll find that knowledge opens all kinds of plot doors you never would have thought of.

Ok, Bob, since you think you know so much, how do we go about doing this the way you suggest instead of just surfing the 'net for our facts?

I can only go by what I've done in the past. I've interviewed and gone on ride-alongs with cops. I've interviewed real life detectives and even one chief of police of a semi-large city. I've bought lunches or visited people at work to watch them in action, all kinds of doctors, forensic scientists, gunsmiths, military experts, lawyers, art experts, theoretical physicists, historians, chefs, FBI agents, theologists, you name it, I went and found them. It's time consuming and a lot of effort, but great scripts are born from these things.

I found all these experts all had the same thing in common. They wanted me to get what I was writing about; their profession or hobby or life, correct. To a person, they mostly hated the way their professions had been portrayed in film and on TV and were more than happy to help me get it right. Did I know all these people before interviewing them or watching them work? Nope. I cold called some of them or got referrals from friends for others and told them I was writing a film about what they do for a living or were experts in and wanted to get it right. A few have said no, but mostly it's been a fabulous experience leading to a couple of lasting friendships.

Great research makes your job, writing a well-crafted story, easier and it helps once you've optioned or sold a script, too. I can think of three separate instances where I was in production meetings getting notes where someone has questioned whether something specific I wrote in the script could really happen. In all three instances I was able to use the research to prove that each thing could and, in most cases, would happen in whatever setting or occupation I set my story. Not only are they impressed that you know, but sometimes stop asking those kinds of questions after a while because you've demonstrated that you do your research.

Yes, it takes more of your valuable time. Yes, you do have to delay starting your script with the great idea. Yes, it takes effort and does cost something, but it also leads to your script being a whole lot better than if you don't. It might make the difference between an option or a pass.

DECIDING ON YOUR STORY

The first question you need to ask yourself after finding a premise and before you do your research for a story that you think will make a great, funny or scary or thrilling script, is to ask:

"Who is my audience for this film?" And if you answer "Everyone", you'd be fooling yourself. Be honest, who do you think wants to see your DEA agent revenge film when nothing like that has been a success in the last 25 years.

Ask yourself, "Is this old, tired, and cliched, or is this fresh and different?" And again, be honest. Finding a unique story is work, but they can come from anywhere and you have to be open to recognizing them as you live your life.

From conversations you hear or have, from articles you read and ask, "What if?" I had a friend tell me a story about something great that happened to his wife and I asked myself, "What if this had not gone so well?" and had a very fresh cool idea for a thriller. I took a nice human-interest story with a sweet ending and made it very scary and twisted by thinking, "What if?".

Look at interesting things around you and twist them. Look at places you visit and make up fun, funny, or scary things that could happen there. Take experiences you've had and turn them on their head.

The last thing you want to do is write another "Wife and daughter are killed, ex-marine who promised he'd never kill again is now out for revenge" movie. No one wants to make this film. You could do "a non-violent ex-marine who finds out his wife is a brilliant serial killer and now he has to stop her himself, after the cops don't believe him", if you want to twist it around a little. It doesn't take much to make an old tired idea fresh. It just takes thought and creativity. Unfortunately, this is something that's missing in 98% of the scripts floating around out there. What you want is your script to be in that 2% that readers will finish reading because it doesn't suck.

I didn't fish that 98% of scripts are terrible number out of thin air either. I got it by talking to producers, agents, managers, screenwriting contest readers, and production company readers who have to look at these scripts every day. A great script is like a rare gem to them. Valuable and not easy to find. The bad script average was 98%. A couple of producers said 99.9%. Yes, it's that hard to write a great script and have it recognized.

The point is, you don't just pick the first idea that comes into your head. You actually think about, do research on, and ask questions about the ideas you come up with. Is this the one that can set me apart from the 98%? Is it fresh? Is it unique?

Which leads me to the next subject when deciding what to write.

CHASING TRENDS

When screenwriters decide their next script will be thematically the same as whatever the latest hit film was, this is not really as good an idea as it seems.

There are loads of so-called experts, including some managers apparently, who think this is the only way for new writers to get themselves out there. Don't write what you're passionate about or what's new and different. Write something that's already been done.

Does that sound like a good way to get your writing noticed or to break in? Producers are looking for the next exciting new writer. How can you be that and write something that's already glutted the marketplace?

To me, trend chasing is an exercise in futility. You understand that films are developed over years. By the time your trend chasing script gets out there, that trend has been replaced by another one or maybe two.

New writers get noticed for their trend setting, not chasing. By their wholly original work, which may never get made, but sets them apart from all the formula drones and trend chasers whose scripts are routinely rejected at the first phase of review.

Like I said earlier, new writers get noticed by their own unique voice, a voice that gets attention instead of yawns or worse, derision when your script is the same as everyone else's. How do you find your own voice if you're trying to write another version of whatever is already out there? You don't. You get thrown into the reject pile or never read because your logline screams: Seen it before.

With everything you see out there on the big screen I can see how every screenwriter who wants their name there would think this was the way. But it's a false flag. The writers whose names appear on those films got them there by first writing something so original that their writing was noticed as something different or special in the first place, that they knew how to tell an original story. That set the writer apart from the masses and got them in the rooms they needed to be in to succeed.

It's not an accident that the most exciting new original stuff is now on streaming platforms. These are ideas and scripts by people not afraid to go out of the box. To write what they're passionate about. Did it take a long time to get there? You bet. It takes everyone a long time to get there. But they did get there. That's the take away. Not by chasing a trend, but by being original storytellers.

The best spec scripts I read are the out of the box, creative storytelling scripts. Amazing from start to finish. Do they get made right off the bat after everyone goes nuts over them in the industry? Nope. They sometimes sit. For years. But those writers can get a career out of that script. It puts them on the map. It gives them instant credibility with decision makers. Copying trends doesn't allow that to happen. You are one of tens of thousands chasing that same trend that's already old and tired by the time your script gets read. You're not the only one doing that by a long shot.

Don't chase trends. No matter what you hear or what "experts" say, you'll always be late to the party. Do the hard work it takes to think of a story that's unique. That you haven't seen before. It might not be successful because, again, truthfully most every script isn't. If that happens, write another one. Then another.

Then another.

QUESTIONS TO ASK BEFORE WRITING YOUR FILM

"Who is my audience?" Everybody is not an acceptable answer.

"Has this been done to death before?" Unless your take on zombies is extraordinary, let it go.

"Is this really just an episode of an old TV show in reruns now?" I see this all the time in scripts.

"What about this would make someone choose to watch it? Is it different enough?"

"When was the last time I saw a cop, hospital, lawyer, FBI, etc., film that got made and was successful?" Clue? 25 years. TV is another thing, but even there, it's harder to do something different in these areas. No one wants to make a film about cops unless it's something way out of the box.

And answer these questions honestly. If you don't like the answers, think of another story.

Screenwriting starts and ends with story.

If you ask 100 producers what they're looking for in a script, 100 will answer...

STORY.

Nothing else matters. That's what you have to have at the front of your mind as you start your script. A story you have confidence is one that will garner interest because of its originality.

Got your story idea? Good. Because now you have to write it.

CHAPTER 4

YOUR CHARACTERS

Now you have your premise, the story you want to tell. And I'm sure you have an idea who the characters in your story will be. If you don't, you should. Make a list of them.

Then, right off the bat, you have to define them in the context of your story. Who are they? What makes them fit for this journey? Who or what wants to stop them or delay them? Who are their friends? Their lovers? Their family? Their adversaries? Who do you need in this story to make it complete?

Then it's your responsibility to get to know them so well that you don't make the huge mistake of having them do something out of character in your story for convenience. That stops a good reader in their tracks and invalidates your whole script in their eyes. It's very important for you to fully understand who the players in your story are so well that you know what they'd do in any situation, even situations not in your story.

You need to understand their personal philosophies. Their emotional make up, their thoughts, even though you can't show those thoughts, their responses to stress or problems, their unique skills, and these are skills you need to establish, not have them instantly know for convenience, their defined breadth of intelligence or lack of it, their wants and needs, and more importantly, why they want or need the things they do.

That's a lot, huh?

You need to treat them like they really exist, because in a film, the audience has to believe they do for them to be successful characters. They have to be fully formed three-dimensional people. This can help prevent, to a certain extent, having them do things out of character or things that real people can't or wouldn't do, that are instant read killers.

Something that can help you with this is to remember that all character actions are either decisions or responses. Just like real life. This is very important. You have to imbue them with decisions and reactions that make sense to their character and to the story. The worst scripts out there are the ones where characters don't act or react like real people in the situations they're put in. Again, this is where good research helps.

You define them before you start writing by giving them a...

BACKSTORY

This is where their personal philosophies, their outlooks, their weaknesses, their strengths, their expertise or knowledge, everything that makes them who they are, comes from. These things do not have to be things you put into the script either, but things that give you a better understanding of who they are.

There are some writers who write full biographies of their characters before they start writing their script. My personal philosophy is new screenwriters should be willing to try different things to see what works for them or what combinations of those things works for them.

Me? I don't write long backstories for my characters because I keep all that stuff in my head. That's my way. Your way might be the exact opposite with everything written down. It's exclusive to each writer. That's where experimentation comes in.

So, if you want to write biographies, do it. Whatever helps you understand what your character will or won't do, can or can't do, and why, in the story you've put them in.

I do write a vivid single sentence describing each character. A description that I do not use in the script, but sometimes use as reference as they get introduced into the story.

I have a writer friend who has interview questions he's come up with for his main characters and answers them in their voice to get a better idea for himself who they are and how they sound. The possibilities of discovery are endless. Do what works for you.

Start with your main characters. Your Protagonist or hero, or anti-hero. They can be anything you want. They just have to be consistent to the reader the way they are defined in your story. If you need to redefine them during the writing process, make sure it resonates through the entire script. If you need to go back through the entire script to make changes, do it. Inconsistency in character is a script killer.

Next, your Antagonist, your villain, if you have one. Remember, an antagonist can be anything, a person, a house, a computer program, the weather, a forest, a bear, an angel, a ghost, a werewolf, they don't always have to be a human, even though most antagonists are.

But whatever your antagonist is, define them before you start. Know who or what they're going to be and what makes them tick. You need an antagonist. Without conflict there is no story. Well, no story anyone wants to see.

After the main characters, you also need secondary characters.

There are three categories of characters: major, secondary, and incidental. Secondary characters are directly involved with the plot, unlike the incidental characters.

A Police Officer that's related to the main character or is integral to the main story or a sub-plot, is a secondary character. The story doesn't exist the way you want to tell it without them. You need to know what makes these characters tick, too. Who they are and how they relate to the protagonist and the antagonist? You can also kill these characters with meaning.

A police officer that shows up at a crime scene and is never seen again is incidental. A parking lot attendant who just parks the antagonist's car is incidental. Incidental characters do not need to be defined.

One thing to remember…these are your characters. They can be anything you want them to be. Anything. Any gender. Any race. You can give them any characteristics you want, as long as they stay consistent. There is no limitation to who or what they can be in your fictional story. They just have to make sense in that story.

CHARACTER ARCS

A character arc is the emotional change in your character from the beginning to the end of your story. If your protagonist has a character arc, they begin their journey in your story as one type of person and gradually transform into a different type of person as they live the adventure of your story. It all depends on the story you're trying to tell. Most protagonists in most scripts have this character arc.

Do they have to?

Nope. They do not. It all depends on the story you want to tell.

In my script *Extracurricular Activities*, the protagonist, Reagan Collins, doesn't have any arc. None. He's exactly the same person he was at the end as he was at the beginning. But everybody else surrounding him in the story? They all have character arcs, some of them extreme, all caused by the decisions and reactions of the unchanging Reagan Collins. I made a conscious decision for him not to arc in this story. He needed not to arc for the film to work.

It's a complex twisted story that I built layer on top of layer, with a lot of thought.

In *The Right Girl,* a film that I wrote with Jeff Willis, our protagonist has a huge arc, only taking three other people on an arc with her, leaving most everyone else in the story unchanged. It wasn't anything we had to decide because the premise of that story was her arc. Without that arc, we had no story.

Both films are successful, despite having the yin and yang of protagonist character arcs.

Your story and your story alone should dictate these arcs. Never try to shoehorn an arc into a story because you think it needs to be there or you've read every character needs an arc. Let the story decide, but also don't fight it.

As your characters arc, these arcs should come as they chase their goal and experience difficulties, then overcome them, fundamentally changing them in some way. You should be able to track the changes in them as your story progresses, watching the conflicts in the story spur each inner change.

One more thing, character arcs don't always have to mean characters change for the better. It depends on your story. Great innovative scripts defy convention. Just because you've been told characters have to do things because it's expected, doesn't mean you have to do that. What you're writing is called an "original" spec script. That word "original" isn't in there for nothing.

REAL LIFE CHARACTERS

What if your characters are based on a contemporary real-life story? Then, again, thorough research is absolutely necessary and key if you want authenticity.

I've written two real life stories. I spent considerable time with the subjects of those stories, because they were still alive, cooperated, and wanted me to get the story right. Those people signed releases for their life rights to me, giving me the legal right to tell their story.

I also interviewed people who knew the subjects of those stories or were actively involved in the story. Those friends and family who were part of their story also signed life rights releases for me.

If the subjects had been deceased, I would have read all I could find about them and researched to see who owned their life rights, if anyone did. You don't tackle stories like this without doing your due diligence.

I'm not going to get into the legalities of writing a real-life story without obtaining life rights for all involved or the book rights, if you're using books for your information, because I'm not a lawyer. I do know you need to get these things squared away if you ever want to sell your script.

It's always in your best interest to consult an entertainment attorney if you have any legal questions about rights. I obtained the life rights before I wrote both scripts, with the help of a lawyer.

If it's a historical character or situation and more than a hundred years old, there are less hoops to jump through, but you still need to square away any questions producers might have on the subject, especially about where you got your knowledge on the subject and specific information. If you used books for that information, did you get the rights to those books?

If it's your own life rights, meaning you're writing something autobiographical, which I do not recommend, you still need to get releases from everyone else involved in your story. Relatives and friends think everyone gets paid millions in the film industry and problems will surface without those releases. Trust me on this.

Why don't I recommend that you write your own life story?

NOBODY WANTS TO BUY OR SEE YOUR LIFE STORY

This is not easy for a lot of people to understand because they really believe their life story would be a great film. But I need to be up front about how producers and reps feel about life story films when it's about someone nobody has ever heard of.

This includes you, unless you're famous or have been in the news in a compelling story that millions saw and have a story that will bring in a pre-sold audience that wants to know more about you than they already know.

The second a writer says, "And it's my life story" in a pitch or query letter, producers and reps can't pass on it fast enough. This is for a lot of reasons, mainly they just aren't movies. There's nothing that makes those stories something an audience would ever pay or choose to see. I understand your life may have been hard or special you to and your loved ones. It's not a movie. Honest.

The second reason? The writer is too close to it and wouldn't be open to all the massive changes producers and directors would make to it. And they would make changes to your true story that weren't true. It's a kettle of fish they don't want to swim with.

If you feel you want or need to write a film based on your life, fictionalize it, take big liberties with it, and never tell anyone it's based on your life. I know one writer that did this successfully. He's still never told the producers or the director.

I'm not saying this to hurt your feelings or make you upset because you know your life story is incredible and the exception. It's not. Producers will instantly pass the second you say it's based on your life.

NAMING YOUR CHARACTERS

Guess what? You get to make up the names. Out of the blue. You can use combinations of friend's names. Family names. Baby name books. Names you hear or see someplace or combinations of them. But, there are a few things you should think about when naming your characters.

1. Don't be cute. Naming a woman who is greedy Penny Pincher is probably not a good thing. Why? It takes the reader out of the story long enough to roll their eyes and that might be long enough to decide to not read any further. Pun names sound like fun, but they're not appreciated. They're just dumb.

2. Unpronounceable names. Hoxrust Huffqunhuffper. Kerfffle Bzzhlteton. You think I'm kidding? I'm not. I've seen them. They're not clever. Do you really want to take the reader out of the story to try and figure out how to say a character's name? I don't think so. Be smart. You can think up names that the reader can read on the page, not cringe at, and be able to say in their head.

3. Don't name all your characters starting with the same letter. Jane, Joe, Josey, Jessie, Jonquil. When on the page, it's easy for the reader to get these characters mixed up if you do this. Make sure your character names are different enough so this doesn't happen.

4. Everybody doesn't need a name. Who? One line, incidental characters. Characters who are part of a scene, then you never see them again. Why can't I give them a name? Because a reader will want to know what happened to Steve, but not to Cop #1. It's better not to name them because then the reader isn't expecting them to come back. Coroner. Woman. Bearded Man. Waitress. It can be a physical description or occupation. If they aren't coming back, don't name them.

One more thing about character names. Don't be too precious about them. They can get changed and often will after selling your script, for all kinds of reasons. So, agonizing over their names doesn't make much sense.

Choose good ones for your story for sure, but they're less important than you think.

Every name in a sold script is vetted by lawyers to see if there really is a Jerry Howitzer in Philadelphia who's a lawyer, like the one in your script. If there is? You have to change the name so you don't get sued. This happens with every important name in your script. Or, the producer decides to name your protagonist after his new grandson. This has happened, too. To me.

Think them out, but don't fall in love with those names.

INTRODUCING YOUR CHARACTERS

The first time your characters appear in your script in an Action Block, you CAPITALIZE, in ALL CAPS, their name. Why? It's shows the reader when that particular character is introduced into the story, so they're not looking back over what they've read already to see if they missed that character and also, later on, this information is used for scheduling.

```
BOB, 30s, walks into the room.
```

After that, you never do it. This goes for every character, even the ones without names.

```
A WAITRESS, 50s, approaches the table.
```

Age is referred to once, when the character is introduced. Age ranges are fine. No one looks exactly 23 in real life.

They look like they're in their 20s. So, 20s works. Specific ages are another thing that can take the reader out of the story. You can, if you want to, use late 20s, early 30s, those work, but ages like 47 just look weird and can stop a reader who has to think, "Why is this character specifically 47?" Not good. If it's a no name character, you can leave the age off, if you want.

It's worth mentioning the exception when the specific age is important. In a biopic where
you're showing the same character at various ages, or when the specific age plays a role in the story, like when it's important that a high school character be over 16 so they can drive, or over 18 so they don't need parental consent. If a character is under 20, a specific age is ok because of the huge experience and personality differences between a character who's 8 and one who is 17.

A character's gender can also be put into the intro if it's not apparent. A character's ethnicity can also be put into their introduction, if you want to. Diversity is a good thing.

```
JULES,    30s,    an    African    American
Attorney, sits behind her huge desk, not
bothering to stand as Caitlin walks into
her  office.  She  removes  her  ornate
reading glasses and looks Caitlin over.
```

When you introduce a character, you can also put a character description, including things that may not be seen by an audience. Yes, I know. Gurus say you can't do this. You can. Keep it to one sentence. Avoid long, detailed character descriptions. This isn't a novel. But these kinds of introductions can help a reader start to understand your character right away.

```
BOB, 30s, walks into the room. He's
unkempt and he looks like he's never met
a pound cake he didn't love.
```

What they wear, the color of their hair, eyes, or anything else, unless it's an important plot point, is not necessary and a waste of storytelling space.

Then there's this.

```
BOBBETTE, 30s, beautiful, the kind of
girl you dream about, with the kind of
luscious, voluptuous body other women
are jealous of and men crave, walks into
the room.
```

I've seen crap like this in scripts a lot, unfortunately. Never do this. Ever.

Why? Unless this kind of beauty is a strong plot point, and there are better ways to write it, this is pandering, sexist, and wrong. We're in the 21st Century now. Join us.

I read a script not too long ago where every female character was described this way, with some extra flourish, to be as sexy and/or beautiful as she could be. It took me right out of the story. If you look around you wherever you are, you aren't going to see a lot of supermodels, so why fill your script with them.

Whenever a reader or producer sees a script full of beautiful sexy women, every physical attribute in detail for no other reason than the writer describes them that way; they stop reading. These kinds of introductions are a relic of the past. Let's keep them there.

You want to write a story that resonates with real people? Make your characters real people. Make the reader see real people. You can put them in unique and other worldly situations, but they still need to be real. Let the reader decide who your characters are inside and out by their dialogue and action. What those readers feel and see in their heads, as these characters come alive.

What your characters do and say in your story should define them without a detailed description anyway. If they don't, you need to rethink your story.

One of the most fun things about creating a story is inventing the characters it's about. If you believe they're alive in the world of your story, so will the reader. This takes a lot of thought and knowing those characters as well as you know yourself.

You want characters the reader or producers or actors want to make come alive on a screen. You do that and you're gold.

CHAPTER 5

DIALOGUE

What characters say in your script that moves your story forward.

One thing before we go any further, every word spoken by your characters needs to be looked at through the lens of the whole story. Does what they say have a direct effect on the story you're trying to tell?

It can be big or the smallest thing, but it has to reverberate through the whole script. One of the worst things you can do is waste valuable white space on the page with dialogue that doesn't move your story.

Then you have to make it sound like real people are speaking. Good realistic dialogue elevates a script and sets it apart. Bad dialogue kills it dead.

This means that your characters also get to speak like real people do. With bad grammar. Incomplete sentences.

Unfinished sentences. One word sentences. Words like, "gonna" and "wanna". Sometimes they can say what they need to with a gesture and no words at all. Just like real people do.

How do you find dialogue like this for your script? How do you develop the ability to write it?

You actively listen to people. Eavesdrop on conversations anywhere you can without looking weird. Take note of how people speak. How they communicate. It's all over the map, but it sounds real, not stilted, like most bad dialogue in scripts. I've listened to conversations at coffee houses, at weddings, on a train, in an airplane, at parties, in hotel lobby bars. The places you can eavesdrop are endless. I've gotten something I can use in each of those places.

This is your job as a screenwriter. This is as much research as your ride along with the police.

There is one big difference between real life dialogue and screenplay dialogue. When you eavesdrop in real life you hear a lot of small talk. In good scripts you hear none of that. Think about it. Every line of dialogue has some character or story advancing meaning. This is your task as a writer. To give your characters realistic meaningful dialogue with the least words possible that only advances the story, but still strikes the reader as so realistic it's like they're the ones eavesdropping, but on conversations meaningful to your story.

Yep. That's a lot to ask. But it's the difference between great screenwriting and scripts that get rejected in the first 10 pages.

Let's see some examples.

Here's a scene where an office worker asks another if he would like to go out for coffee. This is what I see from new screenwriters.

GARY

```
I  need  to  get  of  out  this
place now. Do you want to come
with me for some fancy coffee?
```
                    CHAS

```
I  love  fancy  coffee.  It  would
be  good  to  do  so,  but  I
cannot.  The  Boss  would  not
like  for  me  to  leave  here
before  I  finish  this  report
for him on time.
```

Bad, right? Who talks this way? Bots, maybe? Not humans.

I see dialogue like this in scripts all the time. Why? Zero thought has gone into it. No thought of who the character is, how that particular character would say something based on your definition of them or to how it should advance the story or that it should at least sound like a human being is saying it.

What have we learned about the story or the characters from this exchange? Not a darn thing.

Plus, the dialogue is laughable if it were ever said out loud.

What then, would be better? This?

                    GARY

Hey. I gotta get out of here.
How 'bout some coffee?

                    CHAS

Can't. Boss needs this report.

Sure, if we already know about these characters and we're
trying to get Gary out of the office alone for story purposes,
this works. Short, sweet, real.

But, if we don't know these people or the story yet, it tells
you nothing about them. There's zero information passed to
the audience about who these people are. There's no story
advanced.

Try this…

                    GARY

I didn't get any sleep last
night. Grace is driving me
nuts with all her spending. I
need to talk to somebody.
Wanna go get coffee?

                    CHAS

Wow,   uh,   don't   take   this
wrong, man, but I can't loan
you any more money. If you
just want to talk? Cool. Happy

```
to. But not until I finish
this report.
```

Now we're getting someplace. We know Gary has money problems. He's probably married to a woman named Grace, or she's his girlfriend or he's having an affair, a lot of possibilities here. Maybe his money problems lead Gary to do something that sets our film on its road to being a thriller or a road comedy or whatever you want it to be. But information about the story is now out there with natural sounding dialogue.

And we know Chas has been a good enough friend to loan him money in the past, but isn't that good a friend to do it again. Maybe this will cost Chas his life. Or not.

The original lines? Awful. Not human. Accomplish nothing.

The first rewrite? Simple, to the point, and maybe it works depending on the context. At least the dialogue sounds real. But how does it advance the story, if that's what it needs to do? Or tell us anything about the characters? It doesn't.

Second rewrite? All kinds of information and undercurrents of things maybe to come. Nothing wasted.

And I see a lot of wasted dialogue all the time. What do I consider wasted dialogue?

Small talk is wasted dialogue. A recurring new writer sin. It drives readers crazy. Characters arriving and greeting each other, engaging in meaningless talk before the meat of the scene happens or wasting dialogue with long good-byes or an attempted zingy joke that has nothing to do with the story, ending the scene.

Think about the great scripts you've read. You don't see people saying "Hi. How are you" or the "I'm fine" answers in there. It isn't necessary. It advances nothing. Unless those lines of dialogue serve a purpose, you don't need them. Now go back and look at the dialogue in your scripts. How much small talk is there? You might be surprised.

Read great scripts and you'll see the same thing in all those conversations:

IN LATE, OUT EARLY

This is why in good scripts you see conversations start mid-stream and end before goodbye. You need to look at all your scenes and the dialogue in them and think, "When is the latest I can start this conversation or scene and still get the information out without confusing the reader?"

Yes, sometimes that means deleting fun, funny dialogue you love because it doesn't add anything to the story at the beginning of a scene.

Same at the end of a scene. "How can I end this early and still have it transition seamlessly to the next scene without losing the information I need to get across and also not waste time with stuff that doesn't advance the story". This is what you should be thinking. Not about the joke that was so cool that ended a too long scene.

Ok Bob, can you give me an example? Glad you asked….

This is a scene from my thriller script *A*.

In the scene before this one, we see a man, George, brutally killed in an alley and watch the killer spray paint an *A* in red on George's chest afterward. This scene is what happens next.

But before we get there, let's talk about:

What didn't happen next in the script.

No bystander discovers the body. No one calls the police. No Police Cars or Ambulances are seen arriving. That's all wasted story space, because where the next scene starts, the reader assumes, correctly, that these things already happened in the natural course of things. You don't need to show them. Brevity and efficiency of story.

So, I went from the murder scene to this:

EXT. ALLEY -- DAY

Police tape all around. Multiple official cars and COPS and the

Coroner's wagon. CSU COPS work the scene, cameras snapping.

Two Cops, one young and uniformed, JAKE, late 20s, and one older and plainclothes, MARTIN GRACE, 50s, stand over George's body. The CORONER, 60s, pulls a thermometer out of George's liver and looks at it, then at them.

                    CORONER

No more than 6 to 8 hours. Kinda hard to pin

it down better than that. It was cold last night.

He looks at George's chest and then at Martin.

                    CORONER (CONT'D)
An "A"?

Martin cocks his head and looks again at George's chest.

                    MARTIN
Looks like it to me.

                    CORONER
A red "A". Unbelievable.

                    JAKE
Yeah. I don't get it.

Martin looks sideways at him.

                    MARTIN
You didn't take High School English?

                    JAKE

Wasn't my favorite, but yeah, sure.

Everybody had to. Why?

                    CORONER

Oh c'mon. The Scarlet Letter?

Martin chuckles.

                    JAKE

Ok. I'm lost here.

                    MARTIN

Don't they teach you guys anything

anymore?

He looks Jake in the eye.

                    MARTIN (CONT'D)

The "A" stands for adultery.

                    JAKE

Huh?

                CORONER
Nathaniel Hawthorne just rolled over
in his grave.

                MARTIN
Having an affair? Screwing around
on your wife? Adultery?

                JAKE
Oh. That adultery.

Jake looks at the body. The light bulb
goes off.

                JAKE (CONT'D)
Ohhhhh. He was killed because he --

                CORONER
-- didn't read enough Great American
Literature.
Martin laughs.

                    JAKE

No. Seriously. That could be the
motive here.

The Coroner and Martin both laugh.

                    CORONER

On that note, I'm finished. I leave
the case in the good hands of Sherlock
here.

He points to Jake.

                    MARTIN

I'll give you a holler when you can
get the body out of here.

The Coroner takes his gloves off and
closes his bag.

                    CORONER

I need some caffeine. I'm gonna get
some coffee. You guys want some?

Both cops shake their heads, "No". The
Coroner walks away.

             JAKE
You figured out the motive before I
said anything, huh?

Martin shakes his head, "Yes."
             MARTIN
And speaking of that, we're keeping
the "A" painted on his chest to
ourselves for now. Nothing to the
press or public.

             JAKE
I'll pass it along.

Jake looks at Martin then at the body
again.

             JAKE
Is there a movie version of this
Scarlet Letter thing?

Martin rolls his eyes.

Look where this scene starts. Cops are already there. Coroner is already working on the body. There's no pulling up in cars and getting out. There are no greetings. It starts in the middle of the scene.

Look at what information was given to the reader in the dialogue about the story, what I wanted to accomplish with this scene.

The definition of the Scarlet Letter for anyone who doesn't know. That it was a book. That our Older Detective, Martin is smart, savvy, and patient. That our Young Cop is green. That they're keeping the "A" as a secret from the news and the public.

Nothing in this scene is accidental. It was planned. Doesn't mean you can't discover a more creative way than you planned in the middle of writing, it just means you knew exactly what this scene needed to do to move your story forward in a meaningful way. You should always know this before you write a scene.

Ask yourself after you write it, is my dialogue realistic to these characters? Am I communicating the important information the audience needs in a natural way? Am I getting into the conversation late and out early?

Yes, there's a lot to think about. A lot of balls in the air. It's not easy. Dialogue is, to most, the hardest part to get right. Why? Because it has to sound natural while getting needed exposition out.

BAD EXPOSITION / ON THE NOSE DIALOGUE

What is exposition? It's the important information that your audience needs from your story. Usually it's information your characters already know about each other or situations they are already familiar with. It can be the motivation of an antagonist, something they already know, but the audience doesn't and needs to. Exposition gives them this.

How you convey this exposition can be the difference in your script being read past page 10. Usually bad exposition is conveyed by On the Nose Dialogue.

The worst kind of dialogue. It can be as bad as:

```
EXT. STREET - DAY

Wilson and Betty watch the ball roll
down the street. Wilson points.

                WILSON

That ball is rolling down the street. ←
```
very bad

Yes, that bad. Where the dialogue is telling the reader what they are seeing in the Action Block. I know this seems like it should be common knowledge, but I see it all the time. Here's a clue: You don't need to use dialogue to talk about what the audience is seeing. They know.

Or, On the Nose Dialogue can also be this:

Where information, exposition you need the reader to know for story, like established relationships between characters, jobs, skills, hobbies that might be plot points, motivations, you get the idea, are divulged. Let's choose relationships for this example.

```
INT. KITCHEN - DAY

Felicia and Gwen bake cookies. Felicia
looks at Gwen


                    FELICIA

Remember when we were sisters?
```

Not only is this on the nose dialogue, it's the worst kind of exposition. The writer needs for you to know these two are sisters and thought this would be the best way to communicate it. I know this is extreme, but it's actually a good example of how stupid it can get. Plus, I actually saw this dialogue in a script.

How do you solve bad exposition? People telling each other things they already know about each other and wouldn't talk about or say to each other in real life?

This is the kind of dialogue that destroys a script. But there's an antidote.

SUBTEXT

Subtext is the art of revealing exposition in a natural way, by talking about something else that reveals the truth you need the reader to know. This is the way real human beings speak to each other.

How does this work?

Let's go back to Gwen and Felicia. They're sisters, right? We need the reader to know this. You can say it in their character descriptions, but that doesn't show it to the audience, and you look pretty amateur doing it that way and without finding a way to let the audience know, too.

```
INT.   KITCHEN - DAY

Felicia  and  Gwen  bake  cookies.  Felicia
looks at Gwen.



              FELICIA

Did  you  call  Mom  and  tell  her  the  truth?
I'm  tired  of  running  interference  for
you.
```

Ok. Now we know they're sisters. We know Gwen and Mom are having problems. We know Felicia is the go-between and is exasperated about it. Look at all the exposition in just two sentences. All in subtext. Saying what the reader/audience needs to know without saying it directly or with on the nose dialogue.

Now, let's look at a whole scene of subtext. This is from my script *Albert and Kim* a story of redemption for two very different people thrown together by chance. Kim is a

Korean American. In this scene, a flashback, yes, an evil flashback and yes, if they work for the story you're telling, you can use them, to Kim's youth to see why she's like she is at 20, where the story takes place.

INT. PIANO STUDIO - DAY

MRS. GRANT, 45, sits next to Young Kim, 10, on the piano bench.

In front of them is a full-size grand piano.

                    YOUNG KIM
Thank you for making my mom sit

outside.

                    MRS. GRANT
I do that for all my students.

These lessons are for you. Not

her.

Mrs. Grant places some music in front of Kim.

                    MRS. GRANT (CONT'D)
Your old teacher told me you

outgrew her faster than any other

student. Let's see what you can

do.

She opens the music. Young Kim looks at it
and makes a face.

                    YOUNG KIM
Mozart?

Mrs. Grant takes a moment to size her up.

                    MRS. GRANT
You want to play something else to
show me what you can do?

                    YOUNG KIM
My mother can't hear us?

                    MRS. GRANT
No dear. She's two rooms away in
my waiting area. What's going on?

Young Kim reaches down and picks up her case
and pulls out a
thick book of music with the cover torn off.

                    YOUNG KIM
You won't tell my parents?

                    MRS. GRANT
Honey? What are you so afraid of?

                    YOUNG KIM
I want to play what I like.

                    MRS. GRANT
Well, I teach classical, but we can
make a little wiggle room to play
some pop music if you like.

                    YOUNG KIM
No. I want to play this.

She opens the book to the first page of
music. Mrs. Grant

looks at it hard. Her eyes widen.

                    MRS. GRANT
What is this?

                    YOUNG KIM
Charles Ives, piano sonata no. 2.

                    MRS. GRANT
Oh my God. Where did you get this?

                    YOUNG KIM
The man at the sheet music store
gave it to me and I hid it. It was
playing in the store and I made
friends with it. He saw me.

                    MRS. GRANT
You made friends with it?

                    YOUNG KIM
I make friends with the music I
love. I loved this the minute I
heard it.

                    MRS. GRANT
You can play this?

                    YOUNG KIM

Yes. I practice it on the edge of

my bed with my fingers. I hear it

in my head.

                    MRS. GRANT

Then play it for me. Please.

Young Kim puts her hands on the piano and
brilliantly plays

the dissident difficult piece for a few
moments. Mrs. Grant

places her hand on Young Kim's hands to stop
her.

Young Kim looks at her, confused.

                    YOUNG KIM

No?

                    MRS. GRANT

Oh yes. Very much yes. Someone

like you comes along once in a

lifetime. Yes. I'll talk to your

parents for you. We'll get this

straightened out.

                    YOUNG KIM

No. You can't do that. They'll
find another teacher who'll do what
they say. It can only be their
way. I am to be obedient and learn
Mozart and Bach. If you want to
teach me, you'll have to tell them
Mozart and teach me these.

Mrs. Grant looks at her in wonder.

       MRS. GRANT

How old are you?

Young Kim smiles. She places her hands on
the black and white keys, ready to play
again.

OK. What do we learn about Kim in this scene? That she's a
musical prodigy? Yes. That's she's very intelligent? Oh yeah.
That she's a rebel, even at 10? Yes. That she's single minded and
willing to work hard for what she wants, even in secret?
Absolutely. That's she's willing to lie, even at that young age, to
her parents to get what she wants? You bet. That she understands
the cultural norms she's supposed to adhere to, but wants to be
free of them? Yes.

Now, when we go back to the story with her at 20, all these things
inform her actions from this point on to the reader. The reader
knows all these things about her and there's no more explaining
or exposition to be done about them. She is these things.

All of this is subtext. The conversation between Young Kim and the Piano Teacher is not about what they are actually saying, but about all those things I needed the reader to know about Kim and how ingrained they are to her personality and her personal philosophies.

Also look where the scene started, After introductions. Young Kim is already starting her lesson.

Look where it ends. Instantly, after I get all my subtext exposition out. No fluff.

In late. Out early. Only what pushes the story forward.

OVERWRITING DIALOGUE

One of the things I see a lot in new writer's scripts is overwriting. Too much dialogue. If the audience sees that someone is angry, you don't need your characters to keep repeating how mad they are. Or happy. Or any emotion that shows by physical means on the screen.

Look at what your characters say in every dialogue block. Can one sentence be removed and still say what you want? If so, take one out. I see new writers put that one extra line in all the time. Be the writer who doesn't do that.

I find myself doing that sometimes in some of my first drafts, but by the time I go over the script again, they vanish. It's a hard habit to vanquish.

Try and keep each dialogue block for your characters at a max, three sentences. Most should be 1 or two sentences.

Brevity, once again.

THINGS TO DO TO IMPROVE DIALOGUE

Read your dialogue out loud. You'll be surprised that what you wrote doesn't sound as natural as you thought. It will help you write more natural sounding dialogue in the future.

Do a staged reading of your script. Gather friends, actors, buy them pizza, sit around a table or in a circle and read the script out loud. As the writer, you'd don't do anything but sit in the background with the printed script in your lap taking notes. It can be a game changer in making your script better.

Listen to conversations around you. Everywhere you can. How different people speak.

Remember, your dialogue needs to sound like the reader/audience is doing what I suggest above. Like it's a real meaningful conversation being overheard by a third party.

CHAPTER 6

ACTION BLOCK

Slugline, Action Block, and Dialogue. The bricks you need to stack in the right order to tell your story, writing only what the audience can see and hear.

It's the simplest form of storytelling. And maybe the hardest to get right. Once again, brevity. Ease of read, but still telling your complete story the way you want it seen.

Let's start with what you shouldn't write in an action block. These aren't "rules". They're common sense, considering what a script is.

You shouldn't:

1. Write your character's thoughts. How is the audience going to see this onscreen? I've seen this is action blocks: `"Bob thinks about those wonderful nights with Bobette."` I dare an actor to try and show this with just expressions without being arrested. They can't. Thoughts work in prose. Not here. Don't do it.

2. Describe something that can't be seen. Yes, you can use a sentence to describe your characters when they're introduced, but a lot of new writers overdo it. I've seen this: `"Bob and Bobette in matching jumpsuits from their trip to Guatemala last year, peer into the saltwater fish tank."` Readers see junk like this and it tells them you have no idea what goes into a script.

Ok, then what goes in an Action Block?

Action. Movement. What your characters, props, or the environment they are in, physically do. What you can see and hear them doing.

The environment? Yep. Rain. Tornados. Wind. Animals. Props? Cars, busses, airplanes, screen doors, you get the idea. But mostly your characters physically showing their decisions about or reactions to, their surroundings or the people in those surroundings.

It doesn't have to be fancy either. People can walk, run, fall, sit. It doesn't have to be `"glides into a room like a falcon gently landing on a branch of a tree."` Or `"saunter into the room like a lazy afternoon"`.

Yes, these give an image. But to the typical reader or producer, unless these are accompanied by some pretty great action, story, or characters, they look like the writer is yelling, "Look what I can do".

Please don't misunderstand, using descriptive words other then walk, sit, run, can absolutely work, I do it on occasion, but the more you do it, the less impactful they become when you really need them to be meaningful to the story or the character.

Moderation and brevity is the key.

<u>LEAN and MEAN</u>

The less words you can use to describe action the better. A production executive once said to me, "White space is your friend."

So, what is good screenplay action? What does it look like?

Not like this. This is what new writers do all the time as they scream "look at me". And when you scream "look at me", you're also asking them to stop looking at your story. Not what you want at all.

```
Bob flings the door open and runs
quickly into the room. He slides to a
stop, his shoes squeaking on the slick
floor. He's been here before, but he
acts like he hasn't. He looks high and
low in the room. He needs to find it and
he knows it. Finally, he looks in a far
corner and sees the vase. It can't be,
but it is, and it's already broken into
at least five pieces, spread over three
or four feet of floor, like a porcelain
car accident. He stares at this for a
few seconds, not believing what he sees,
then rubs his eyes, shakes his head, and
finally lowers it, crushed, knowing he
is too late.
```

Readers look at paragraphs like this and rub their eyes and shake their heads. If you want to write like this, screenwriting isn't for you. Be a novelist. An action block in a script needs to move the story. How does "porcelain car accident" do that? It doesn't.

Let's look at how an experienced screenwriter might write the above.

```
Bob  runs  into  the  room  and  abruptly
stops.  His  head  swivels,  his  eyes  dart
around,  then  stop,  focused.  There  it  is,
in  the  corner.

The  vase.  Broken.

His  head  lowers.  Defeated.
```

Lots of white space, but you get a clear picture of the action. This is what producers want. To be able to clearly read what is happening with the fewest words possible.

First paragraph,118 words

Second paragraph, 31 words.

Both describe exactly the same action. Both show exactly the same thing on screen. That's what's important. The visual picture doesn't change with less words and is actually more powerful that way.

But there are differences. One lets the reader get on to the next part of the story. One keeps the reader from getting there for a while, slogging through unnecessary words.

A few more paragraphs like the first one and they put your script down and start the next one in the pile they need to read that weekend.

This is extreme, but it makes the point. Don't skimp on the action you need to tell your story, just convey it efficiently.

You can still draw emotions from the reader, but those real emotions need to come from the story itself and not from you using a lot of extra words and word pictures to try and evoke it or manipulate it.

Good readers know the difference.

One other thing about Action Blocks, there's a lot of bad advice from gurus out there that this

```
Bobette,   frustrated,   runs   her   hand
through  her  hair,  pulling  it  a  little.
```

is telling an actor what to do and if you do things like this in your script, actors will be offended. I always ask, "What's this actor's name?" They answer, "I have no idea." I say, "That's right, because there are no actors yet." Nobody is going to be offended. I'm an actor. I've read hundreds of scripts. The only ones that offended me where the ones that wasted my time by being bad.

You are painting a picture in your spec script for the reader to see. A full film to see in their head as they read. Your characters need to do physical things in your story to show their emotions. It all can't be done with dialogue.

What works better in the visual medium of film?

```
Bob  slams  his  fists  on  the  table  in
anger.
```

Or

```
                         BOB
```

I'm so angry.

This is where the ridiculous "Don't tell the actor what to do" advice is completely at odds with writing a good well told story that the reader sees in their mind theater.

There are no actors, just your characters and you may have your characters do all the things you need them to do in action blocks to tell your story visually, from the biggest things to the smallest.

Long blocks of dialogue back and forth are also daunting to readers, as they can take away from the story you're trying to tell by not giving the reader anything to see while the dialogue is going on. That's why it's good to break them up with physical action. Movement.

This is the opening scene from Albert & Kim. First without any action to break up dialogue.

```
EXT. ALLEY - DAY

CARD: 1947 - New York

A seedy dead-end alley. A couple of BUMS
huddle around an old rusty oil barrel
with a fire spouting from it, warming
themselves and drinking cheap wine from
a bottle.

Around the corner, from the street, runs
a ten-year-old
African American boy, YOUNG ALBERT
MOORE. He runs right by
the Bums full speed headed to the end of
the alley.
```

                    BUM
Hey kid, what's the hurry? Slow
down.

                    YOUNG ALBERT
Can't. I'm getting my sax today.
Gonna be a jazz player.

                    BUM
Saxophone? You want a saxophone?
Why we got one right here. Sell it
to you for a fin. Come see it.

                    YOUNG ALBERT
You all just wanna steal my money.

                    BUM
What's a little toad like you want
with a saxophone anyways?

                    YOUNG ALBERT
I told you. Gonna play me some
jazz.

                    BUM
He's a regular Louis Armstrong.

                    YOUNG ALBERT
Louis Armstrong plays the trumpet,
dummy. I'm gonna play like Coleman
Hawkins or Lester Young. Tenor
sax.

                    BUM
Who you callin' dummy? C'mere, you

pipsqueak.

The Bum advances on Young Albert. Young
Albert turns and
runs toward the end of the alley as fast
as he can. The Bum
laughs and returns to the oil can.

It's ok. Conversation. You get the idea. Let's see it with
action breaking up the dialogue. This is what's in the script.

EXT. ALLEY - DAY

CARD: 1947 - New York

A seedy dead-end alley. A couple of BUMS
huddle around an old rusty oil barrel
with a fire spouting from it, warming
themselves and drinking cheap wine from
a bottle.

Around the corner, from the street, runs
a ten-year-old
African American boy, YOUNG ALBERT
MOORE. He runs right by
the Bums full speed headed to the end of
the alley.

                BUM
Hey kid, what's the hurry? Slow
down.

Young Albert skids to a halt and turns to the bums.

                    YOUNG ALBERT
Can't. I'm getting my sax today.
Gonna be a jazz player.

The Bums look at each other, eyes meeting.

                    BUM
Saxophone? You want a saxophone?
Why we got one right here. Sell it
to you for a fin. Come see it.

Young Albert sticks his hand in his pocket, protectively.

                    YOUNG ALBERT
You all just wanna steal my money.
                    BUM
What's a little toad like you want
with a saxophone anyways?

                    YOUNG ALBERT
I told you. Gonna play me some
jazz.

The Bum looks at his friend.

                    BUM
He's a regular Louis Armstrong.

The Other Bum laughs. Young Albert rolls
his eyes, putting
his hands on his hips.

                YOUNG ALBERT
Louis Armstrong plays the trumpet,
dummy. I'm gonna play like Coleman
Hawkins or Lester Young. Tenor
sax.

                BUM
Who you callin' dummy? C'mere, you
pipsqueak.

The Bum advances on Young Albert. Young
Albert turns and
runs toward the end of the alley as fast
as he can. The Bum
laughs and returns to the oil can.

It's not a lot, but enough to paint a much better picture in
the mind of the reader of exactly what's going on in this
scene and it breaks up a long block of dialogue that isn't as
effective without the added action.

Or, you can use action/movement to break up a single
speech. Here's a scene from the script of my film
Extracurricular Activities.

EXT. CEMETERY - WALLACE FAMILY FUNERAL -
DAY

There's a big CROWD at the funeral. Lots
of high school kids,
friends, and family.

Up front are BEN WALLACE, 17, sharp,
impeccably dressed, and
BECKY WALLACE, 16, short, fat,
depressed, and not that smart.

Reagan stands with Ben and Becky. Cliff
looks on from the crowd.

Ben walks to the microphone. He clears
his throat.

                BEN
What can I say about my mother and
father? Free spirits? Definitely.
Adventurous?
Something you all know. One day they're
here
and the next day, gone, who knows where.
Not even
a word from them. Weeks. Sometimes
months.
But then, they always came back. Just
not this time.

One long piece of dialogue. Here the reader pictures Ben as a talking head, just hearing, well, actually reading, what he said, not seeing what I wanted seen to accompany the dialogue and advance the story.

It evokes no emotions. It's not funny.

So now let's look at the scene the way I wrote it in the final shooting script. No talking head here.

EXT. CEMETERY - WALLACE FAMILY FUNERAL - DAY

There's a big CROWD at the funeral. Lots of high school kids, friends, and family.

Up front are BEN WALLACE, 17, sharp, impeccably dressed, and BECKY WALLACE, 16, short, fat, depressed, and not that smart.

Reagan stands with Ben and Becky. Cliff looks on from the crowd. Ben walks to the microphone. He clears his throat.

                    BEN
What can I say about my mother and father?

He stops to compose himself.

                    BEN
Free spirits? Definitely. Adventurous? Something you all know.

His voice breaks a little.

                    BEN
One day they're here and the next day, gone, who knows where. Not even a word from them. Weeks. Sometimes months.

He sighs, lowering his head.

                    BEN
But then, they always came back.

He wipes a tear away.

                    BEN
Just not this time.

I broke up the speech with Ben's physical actions, his reactions to what he was saying, so the reader could get the full picture of what is happening. To see and hear this scene in their head. The actor who played Ben did all these actions as he gave this speech in the film. He wasn't offended it was there. And he's funny doing it.

It becomes a complete picture of what's happening. Not a long block of dialogue on the page where you read words and don't see anything.

Same thing goes with offending directors by "directing a scene". No, you don't put camera moves like:

Camera pans up from Alex's shoes, up his pant legs, to reveal him.

This takes the reader out of the story to a film set where there's a camera. This is a spec script. There are no cameras yet, or directors to offend, by the way, but you can do this.

A pair of dress shoes walk into the room. Claire looks at them, then up at the shoes' owner, ALEX, 30's. He smiles. She waves.

Same action. The picture you want the reader to see is there without the distraction of having the reader imagine the camera. This can be done with any camera shot. All it takes is a little creative thought.

THE DREADED "WE SEE"

You are going to read all kinds of scripts, even scripts from well-known professional writers, where the writer uses "We see…" in the action block. You're going to hear Writing gurus fainting across the land just thinking about this affront to their sensibilities.

My take on "We see"?

I don't use it unless it absolutely fits what I'm trying to do in an action block. If you're writing an amazing story, no one is putting your script down because you've used it. I think I've used it three or four times total in the dozens of scripts I've written. Including one that got produced.

That said, it can be a crutch for new writers, one they can lean on way too much, so my advice is to not use it. You don't need it and it's just extra words that take up white space.

But honestly, no one is clutching their chest and screaming if they see one or two of them in a script. Unless the script sucks, then it doesn't matter anyway.

FIGHT SCENES / CAR CHASES / GUN BATTLES – ACTION SET PIECES

Action set pieces are those big long action scenes you see at least three to four times in action/adventures, but can be in comedies, horror, westerns, war films, you get the idea. You know what they are. You've seen enough of them.

You write what you want the reader to see. Your film. You don't overwrite, but if there are key things you have created and want in your action set pieces, put them in. Show the sequence of events you want to happen. It's your story, you get to do that.

Writing,

```
EXT. ALLEY - DAY

Bob and Bobette fight. Bobette wins.
```

is the height of lazy un-creative writing. Yet, there are writing gurus who say this is acceptable. It's not. Not even close.

Yes, I have heard "You let the stunt coordinator do his/her job." This is ridiculous. First, as you now know too well, there is no stunt coordinator. Secondly, the reader is taken so far out of the script, they may not find their way back. There is nothing for them to see in their imagination.

What does an action set piece look like?

From my spec script, *The Page*. A set piece that really moves the story forward and is exciting at the same time. Look at all the decisions and reactions by everyone, while serious action takes place. Look at the action blocks. Short. Tight. But you can see the action in your head.

```
INT. DRUG STORE - DAY
```

Small independent drug store. In a center aisle, Peter and Gloria look at the shelves. No one inside but them.

                    GLORIA
Ah-ha.

She bends to grab an aspirin bottle off a lower shelf. As
she bends, the red targeting spot from a laser site shows
on the cough medicine that sits on the shelf she was
standing in front of.

Peter sees this, but it takes a second for it to register.
She begins to stand back up.

                    PETER
No!

He tackles her to the floor as gunshots hit the
bottles, spilling cough syrup all over them.

                    PETER
Someone's shooting at us.

She looks at him, blankly. Pissed.

                    PETER
Ok. Me. They're shooting at me.

Another shot hits the bottles spilling more medicine on them.

Gloria pulls her gun.

> GLORIA
> Stay behind me.

She crawls down the aisle.

> PETER
> I thought this was over. I thought
> you caught the mole. Ferdinand said
> that guy was the mole.

She turns her head and looks at him.

> GLORIA
> Would you shut up!

> PETER
> But I thought-

> GLORIA
> Whoever Kennedy was working for
> followed him to the dentist and then
> followed us here. Ok? My fault. I
> should have been looking for it.

> PETER
> Stasi?

The bell on the door to the drug store
jangles as someone
they can't see enters the store. Gloria
holds her finger up
to shush Peter. They hear German spoken
in hushed tones.

                    GLORIA
                    (whispering)
Yep.

She peeks around the corner of the aisle
and holds up two
fingers to him.

She points to her gun, then at Peter. He
feels around his
waist, then grimaces. He whispers to
her.

                    PETER
I left it in the car.

She rolls her eyes and whispers back.

                    GLORIA
I'll distract 'em and you find
something to protect yourself.

She kneels in the aisle, then pops up
and fires a few shots
at the two heavily armed men, the
GERMANS, at the front of the store.

They duck, then stand and return heavy
automatic fire.

Gloria ducks down as items above her are
shredded by the
heavy fire.

Peter crawls quickly down the aisle to
the back of the store.

The shooting stops. Gloria pops up and fires again, hitting
one of the Germans in the arm. He yells and goes down. His
Partner fires again.

Peter, at the back of the store, sees Gloria
on the floor covering up as more items fall on her. As soon
as the shooting stops, she reloads a clip and begins to crawl
back down the aisle to him.

> GLORIA
> See if you can get into the pharmacy. I'll cover you.

Peter sees a Dutch door leading to the pharmacy area.
The top of it is open. He crouches for a second, then runs
low toward it. Gloria stands and fires at the Germans.

Peter dives through the open top of the Dutch door.

INT. DRUG STORE - BACK PHARMACY AREA - DAY

Peter hits the tile floor hard and slides into the shelving,
knocking bottles of pills down on him.

In pain, he looks around and sees the PHARMACIST cowering on the floor. Peter gets up to a crouch.

The Pharmacist holds a full syringe out in front of him
as a weapon.

                    PHARMACIST
Stay away from me. Get away.

                    PETER
It's ok. It's ok. I'm with the FBI.
Is there a back way out of
here?

The Pharmacist relaxes a little.

                    PHARMACIST
What's happening?

                    PETER
No time to explain. You need to get
out of here. Now.

There's more gunfire in the store. Both men duck down
again.

It stops. The Pharmacist points to a door.

                    PHARMACIST
The alley is out there. Will I be
safe?

                    PETER
Safer than in here.

Peter looks at the needle in the
Pharmacist's hand.

                    PETER
What's that?

                    PHARMACIST
Brevital. Only thing I could think
of.

                    PETER
What's it do?

                    PHARMACIST
Quick knock out.

Peter reaches out.

                    PETER
Give it to me and get out.

The Pharmacist hesitates for a second,
then hands it to Peter.
More gunfire from inside. Peter looks at
the Pharmacist.

                    PETER
Go!

The Pharmacist scurries across the
floor, reaches up, opens
the door and is gone.

Peter stares at the open door. More
gunfire from the store.
He looks back toward the store, then
back to the door.

                    PETER
I'm sorry Gloria. I can't do this.

He runs out the door.

EXT. DRUG STORE - BACK ALLEY - DAY

Peter stands in the alley a moment,
unsure. More gunfire is heard from
inside. He runs down the alley.

EXT. DRUG STORE -- DAY

Peter runs to Gloria's car, unlocking
the doors with the
fob. He opens the door, throws the
syringe on the passenger
seat, gets into his car, and starts it.

As he's backing it out, he looks through
the bullet riddled window at the front
of the store to see Gloria, her hands
up, surrendering to the two Germans.

She gets down to her knees. They raise
their guns.

                    PETER
Oh God. I can't-

Peter slams the car into drive and rams
it through the front of the store,
shattering the glass window and hitting
one of the
Germans, throwing him in the air.

He bounces off the hood and on to the floor.

The other German jumps out of the way, hitting the ground,
losing his gun. It clatters across the floor. He makes eye
contact with Gloria, also on the floor.

Gloria jumps to her feet and runs for the gun. The German,
wounded in the arm earlier, lunges after her, tripping her.
She goes down, hard.

The German scrambles to her and grabs her hair, pulling her
to him, as she screams. She tries to punch him in his bleeding arm and gets in one good shot. He yells.

INT. GLORIA'S CAR - DAY

Tossing the airbag aside, Peter sees the syringe at his feet
on the floor. He grabs it and gets out of the car.

INT. DRUG STORE - DAY

The wounded German has his hands around Gloria's throat,
choking her. Peter grabs him and jams the syringe in
the German's neck, injecting it.

The German continues to choke Gloria for a few seconds, then
wobbles and falls over, out cold. Gloria gasps
for breath. Peter moves to her and lifts her up in his arms.

> PETER
> I'm sorry. I'm sorry.

> GLORIA
> Sorry?

> PETER
> I was leaving. I snuck out the back.
> I was gonna steal your car and
> disappear. I was free.

He pulls her close her.

> PETER
> I saw you through the window, with them, and I
> couldn't do it. I couldn't leave you like that.

She musters up a smile.

> GLORIA
> Give me your cell.

> PETER
> What?

> GLORIA
> We have to call Foster and get this mess cleaned up.

He hands her his cell.

                    PETER
I don't get a thank you?

                    GLORIA
Later. Promise.

She starts to dial the cell.

All the action and dialogue are brief enough to get the idea of what's happening. No one in a situation like this is going to have anything but very short sentences to say anyway. In bad scripts, in situations like this, the characters talk too much, they're too glib in dangerous situations unless it's a comedy, and the bad guys always have something expository to say.

In this situation, I chose, on purpose, for them not to say anything but a couple of German phrases when they come in the door. You find out the reason for this later. Nothing written in a scene should be by accident. Everything needs to be planned so you can get those things you need to be there, your plot points that come back to pay off, in the most efficient, yet cinematic way possible. Simple. Effective.

The reader gets to fill out whatever details they want in their head, like you did I hope, reading it.

Yes, this is out of context, so you don't know the story, or the people they referenced, but whoever has read up to this point does and is hopefully drawn in further to the plight of this guy and the woman who is using him for her own ends.

The main plot point here is, he had the chance to get away. To free himself from an impossible situation, but chose not to because of his growing feelings for her. This is incredibly important to the next part of the story. In fact, the rest of the story hinges on the fact that he couldn't leave her.

All the while, I got to stage a cool gun battle, a car hurtling through a window, and our protagonist doing something brave, which up to this point he hasn't been able to do.

The takeaway here: Moderation. Brevity. Again.

Purple prose is for your novels, for the poetry you write a loved one, not for your script.

Keep your action and descriptions tight, but still get in the visuals you need to tell your story.

CHAPTER 7

FORMULA/ACT STUCTURE/WRITING METHODS

I'll make this clear right off the bat. I don't really believe in formula or structure "rules". Period. three act structure can be a good guideline for new writers, but formula? A big false hole that can suck you in, wasting your time.

There are tons of formulas out there. These formulas are where new writers start hearing about the "rules" they must follow or readers will put down their scripts, screaming and swearing. That readers have a check list that tells them where certain story elements, such as Inciting Incidents, Turning Points, Rising Action, Falling Action, and Conflict have to be in your story at certain points in your script and if one is missing, or heaven forbid in the wrong place, they throw your script into a flaming barrel then send you back the ashes.

Some of these formulas can get very specific on the exact page numbers where these things have to take place, or else.

You can relax, there is no "or else".

Good producers, meaning the ones that actually make films, pay no attention to these formulas. Most have no idea they exist because, in the real world of filmmaking, they don't. In all the years of writing for producers and directors and production execs, not a single one has brought any of these formulas or formula books up.

This doesn't stop the gurus from endlessly pontificating on their made-up rules. Depending on who the guru is, there are five elements of story or 7, or, 8, or 12 or…infinity. And more importantly, if you follow their formula, this check list of elements and where they exactly need to go in your story, you will write a great script that producers won't be able to resist. The secret of writing a flawless script. Or so they say. Each one of them. For their own formula.

Yes, the elements I listed are part of storytelling. They exist in some way in every good story. The only one you need to seriously think about while writing is conflict. Without conflict there is no story. Yes, rising action is a thing. Yes, turning points are things, but they exist naturally in good story without you having to shoehorn them in artificially.

Before I get any further, let's talk about the screenwriting "rules" you hear all the time. The "rules" you get warned about time and again from people who never made a film.

When you were young, your parents had rules. Who made them? Your parents. You knew who made them. They had the power to make them and you knew they were real.

The DMV has rules. They have books full of them. You want to drive a vehicle? You need to observe these rules. They're written down in one official place for you to look them up. They are concrete rules you need to obey to officially obtain and retain your driving privileges. You know who made them. You know where to find them. You have to obey because they are laws.

Screenwriting rules? C'mon.

Do you think producers think about these guru invented story rules for one second while reading a script? Oooo, the inciting incident was on page 12 not on page five, so this script is rejected! Or, the inciting incident obviously happened before the first page, REJECTED. Or the protagonist has no arc. Nope, they're looking at the story as a whole. Is this a good story, well told, or not? Period.

They read those first ten pages, not saying to themselves, "Where's the inciting incident?" because they don't care. The story itself either hooks them or it doesn't. Again, you can use story elements as guidelines if you need to, but you can use them any way that works for the story you're telling.

But I'll get in trouble if I do that, Bob. I need to stick to the "rules."

No, you'll write predictable boring stories nobody wants. The truth is:

You get to write your story any way you want.

There. I said it. I will again.

You get to write *your* story any way you want.

There are no rules. Can you use the elements of story as guidelines to make sure your story is as good as you think it is? Sure. You can do anything you want.

There's no group of Hollywood Rule Makers meeting yearly at the Starbucks on Ventura Blvd to pontificate on what the new "rules" are for that year, although again, some of the screenwriting gurus would like you to believe this.

I've been asking for years for someone to show me the official rule book. Nobody has been able to. Why? C'mon. Think about this logically. Not with emotion, which unfortunately a lot of new screenwriters let govern their decisions.

It doesn't exist.

The only thing that matters is story. Is this a great original story readers and producers want to read to the end? Did you write something they haven't seen before, or something they have, in a brand-new way? It's no more complicated than that. Not easy, but no more complicated.

So, now we come back to the guaranteed Hollywood screenplay formulas out there. You do this exactly as we say and you have a sure-fire Hollywood script. Right?

No, of course you don't. You have a script that's just like the thousands of writers who followed the same formula. You think readers or producers don't recognize this? They do and they hate it. And again, thinking logically; if these formulas actually worked, wouldn't there be tens of thousands of great scripts out there because they followed these formulas?

Here's a clue. There aren't. Why? Because they stifle originality. They make a writer write in a box. In some cases, a small box. You have to tailor your story to fit the formula. You're no longer thinking about your story, but how you can construct it and change it to fit what you've been told are expectations. How can you be creative in this matrix?

They also don't take into account that each great story has to be constructed its own way to become a unique original screenplay.

New writers break out when they're original. When they use their creativity and skill to write an out of the box story. Nobody recognizes a writer who is part of the big formula pack out there. How can you stand out writing to a formula? You can't. Plus, those formulas fool you into thinking you don't have to write anything innovative because if you just follow them no matter what you're writing, you'll succeed.

Can you tell I don't like formulas?

Are there things in those formulas that do work? Sure. But those are story elements that are automatically contained in a great story in any order you want to put them.

Think: No limits.

Is three act structure formula? Do I adhere to the three act structure? Yes, in my own way. I believe a good story has three natural acts. It's basic storytelling. Do I personally think about that as I write? No. I don't. I look at my overall story and just write it. When I'm asked where my act breaks are in any of my scripts, I always say, "Wherever you think they are," and then agree with whatever they tell me. My concentration is overall story. That's my only thought as I write.

Should you think about three act structure? If you are just starting out and you need the comfort of a structure, then yes, you should think about your acts as you put your story together.

THREE ACT STRUCTURE

The three act structure has been around since cave painting days, since people sat around a fire and told stories as the only form of entertainment. It's nothing new. Start/Middle/End. If you write a great story not thinking about them, they'll still be there when you're done because it's inherent storytelling.

The first act of a screenplay accomplishes a few things, the introduction of your characters, what their problems or conflicts are going to be, and what happens that starts your protagonist's story or adventure. Yes, this is the inciting incident. Does it need to take place in the first three pages? No, it doesn't, if that's what you need for your story to work. In my film *Extracurricular Activities* the inciting incident happens before the story starts. Did it make a difference? Did producers stop reading and look back to find it? No, they didn't. They wanted to read forward to see what happened next. They were caught up in the story. Also, my main protagonist had no arc. He learned nothing. He didn't grow or change. Guess what? Nobody cared. Why? Because the story had them guessing all the way to the twisted ending.

Your first act needs to hook readers quickly. Just like I talked about the need to be "In late/Out early" in scenes, you also need to do this to start your screenplay. You can't spend the time you can in prose to build characters or set the scene, you need to get directly to your story or you'll never hook the reader.

So, in your first act it's crucial for you to jump start your story. It doesn't have to be instant action either. It can be, depending on what you're trying to do, a conversation between a father and a son or it can start in the middle of a chase down a crowded sidewalk. As long as it's the latest you can get into the story you're telling.

The first ten pages can make or break your script for the reader. Those pages either entice them to read further or they put it down for good. I know this seems unfair, but no matter what you hear, this is how they get through the massive amount of scripts they have to read to find that one jewel.

Your second act is where your protagonist has the bulk of their conflicts. What obstacles they have to overcome on their journey to the end of their story. Does each obstacle have to be worse than the last? No. They can be whatever you choose them to be for your story.

The second act is also where relationships build and overcome conflicts, too. Big and small.

A natural second act has rising action / conflict leading to…

Your third act, where you have the biggest conflict or climax and the resolution of your story. Can your resolution be anything you want? You know the answer now. Yes. It's your story. Does there need to be a big twist ending? Absolutely not. Unless you've spent the whole script setting the reader up for the twist, then you'd better not. There's nothing worse than a twist ending out of nowhere. An ending where the reader can't look back and see all the clues you left that they missed.

This sounds complex, huh? A lot to think about. Like a juggler keeping balls in the air. It is, only the screenwriter keeps about 40 of them in the air as they construct their story.

How do screenwriters keep track of all this? Some of them outline, some write a synopsis, some write a full treatment, or use bullet points. Or none of those. Or a combination of them. Any way you slice it, there's thought, planning, research, and work. And the time it takes to do it well.

The thing to remember, even if you are needing to construct separate acts, the three act structure is flexible. You get to expand and contract it as needed to tell the story you want to tell. It's not a rigid structure no matter what you hear.

So, if you're going to use three act structure to help guide your story, experiment with different ways to get there. Try outlining. Try index cards. Try bullet points. This is a long game. You have time to do these things to get to your own comfort zone.

Creative writing is just that, the freedom to create anything you like, using whatever tools are at your disposal. There's no right or wrong way to get there as long as you get there.

I look at social media on screenwriting boards and all the time there's a post asking, "Can I do this in my story?" The answer is YES. You don't need permission to do anything.

OUTLINES/SYNOPSIS/TREATMENT

Many writers outline their stories, build the whole thing in outline form before they write their screenplay. To some, this is the only way. You write your scene headings and then what happens in that scene, in order, until your story is told, it's laying your whole movie out, without the dialogue.

Like this:

```
INT. GARAGE - DAY

Bob inspects the damage to his car. The
Mechanic tells him how bad it is and how
much it will cost. Bob asks if the trunk
still works. The Mechanic pops it open.
There's a dead body inside. It's Bob's
boss.

EXT. STREET - DAY

Bob runs out of the Garage and down the
street as fast as he can.
```

And so on, for the whole film.

Your outline can also be each scene on a 3x5 card with what you want out of each scene and the characters involved. Even on color coded cards for each act, if you need to. A lot of writers use these as their outline.

Outlines can be in the form of a short story, anywhere from 10 to 50 pages. At the 30 to 50 page range it becomes a TREATMENT. In the treatment, you tell the story and use some of the dialogue you might use in the script. It's a true short story with every plot point spelled out to the ending. You know what a short story looks like.

Any way you choose, it's a *lot* of work to do well, to construct a story that works cinematically. This is why you need to choose your premise carefully. Putting this much work into a premise that's dead on arrival doesn't make good sense. Writing a great script is hard work. Great scripts aren't thrown together. They're meticulously planned and executed.

I do not outline. I never have. Because I love the adventure of creative discovery as I write. I found that it's the best way for me. I have outlined a couple of times, but found I deviated from it about page 12 both times because the story and the characters took it in a different and more desirable direction away from the outline, to better tell the story I wanted to tell.

BULLET POINTS

And there's bullet points, where the writer lists, in my case when I do it, on yellow legal pads, the plot points in the order you want to write them scene by scene.

Bob complains about his boss to Bobette

Bob goes to the company lot and gets in his car and leaves work.

Bob gets hit by Big Black SUV, hit and run.

Bob takes the car to a Garage, Finds his Boss' body in the trunk

Bob runs for his life.

There you go. The next five scenes in the order I need to write them for this story. You can do each act or the whole film or however many scenes you want at a time as you write. Your choice.

SYNOPSIS

Whether you outline or write a treatment or bullet point, at some point you will need a synopsis of your script. A synopsis is a one to three page distilling of your story with no dialogue. The condensed version of your story, hitting all the high points of your plot. You do not have to give away your ending in a synopsis.

Why will you need a synopsis? For producers who option your script to give to finance people who don't want to read a script. I get asked for one every time I option or sell a script. Sometimes before. You need one by the time you want to show your script and having one ahead of time doesn't hurt you.

Sometimes a synopsis alone is enough for some writers to start the script. I've been hired to write films with only a three to ten page synopsis as a guide. Sometimes a producer or a production company will have their own idea for a film and that's all they have.

Outline, treatment, index cards, bullet points, synopsis. Try them all. See what works best. Or what combo of them works.

One thing for sure, I don't believe in the vomit draft. The "write until you're done and don't look back" version of a first draft. Some say "just take notes" and revise in your first rewrite, get that first draft out no matter how bad it is.

My problem with that is, if you're anything like me, the notes are never as clear as they would be if you just went back and implemented them when they were fresh in your mind. It might take you longer to get your first draft done, but it'll be a better script for it. It works for me. I get a lot of credit for having very good first drafts and that's a good thing when you're working for producers. They don't like "vomit drafts" at all.

THAT SAID:

I have been asked what my personal writing method is quite a few times, in magazine interviews, on numerous podcasts, on social media, because new writers want to know what produced writers do. What their method is.

So ok, fair enough....

I start with my premise. A well thought out premise.

How do I find the premise? A lot of "what ifs," based on something I saw or heard, someplace I went, a story someone told to me. I'm always on the lookout for them. I consider a lot of them and throw a lot of them out because I put them through my interrogation questions. Who's the audience? Who'd buy tickets or choose to see this? Has it been done before and if so, what new can I add to it so it's not the same? I'm very hard on my own ideas because it's a lot of hard work to write a script from the ground up and I want it to be viable and not dead on arrival, like a lot of first time writer's scripts are because they didn't do this.

So now:

I have my basic storyline. My premise. I write down a list of the characters I know I'll need to tell it. My protagonist or multiple protagonists depending on the story. My antagonist. I'll name them using the tried and true method of making them up. I think about some of the secondary characters I might need, but usually I find those as I write.

Then, I look at the aspects of this story I know nothing about and start my research. I do what I preach. I go visit people. I interview people on the phone. I use the internet to get information, but double check everything. If it's something I can do myself, I go out and do it, and I do all of these things while taking reams of notes on my trusty yellow legal pads.

Example: I wrote a script where one of the protagonists worked in a commercial bakery making a very specialized baked product. I looked all over the area I live and found that no big commercial bakery within reasonable travel made this specialty item.

So, I got on the internet, found the item and the biggest bakeries in the country making them. They were all in the Midwest states. I ordered some of the items. Yes, I paid out of my pocket for these baked goods. After getting them, tasting them (oh yum), and having others taste them, I called a couple of these companies, asked to speak to their PR people, explained who I was, what I was doing, and who I was writing the screenplay for…

Both of them jumped right on it. I got reams of information on every step of baking this item and how giant bakeries work. Both offered free pastries. When I informed them that I had already actually bought the goods from them, they wanted to help more. I had all the information I needed to write intelligently about this process, so I could add authenticity to the story. And it also helped in adding some pretty funny scenes I never would have had if I hadn't known these things. Yes, this film was produced. *Christmas in Love* on the Hallmark Channel.

Once I do my research and I'm satisfied, I come up with the ending to the film. A *rock solid* ending that will never change as I write the script. I never start a script without knowing the ending. Neither should you. Goals in writing are important. That unchanging ending gives you a writing goal and gives your characters a road they have to stay on to get where they have to be by the end of the story. This can help the new writer from getting lost as they write their script. You know the path you're on and where it's leading at all times.

Then I meticulously plan out the first 10 pages. I can take a few days doing this. Those pages have to grab the reader and hold them so they want to read on to page 11 or 15 or 47, or all the way to the end. Which is your ultimate goal. 98% of read scripts out there don't reach this goal with producers. Established writers understand the vital importance of those first 10 pages.

You have to:

Introduce your main character, who and what they are, set up the whole story, and start it. Give the reader insight into their personality and do it quickly without bad exposition.

Here's the first page and half of my script: *Emotion Sickness*, where you learn a lot about my character, Bob, and how that information helps jump start the story.

EXT. MODERN OFFICE BUILDING -- DAY

People hustle in and out of the
building.

INT. OFFICE - HALLWAY - DAY

Two people, SALESMAN 1 AND SALESMAN 2,
walk down the wide
hallway with their coffee cups in hand.

                SALESMAN 1
So, did they win or not?

                SALESMAN 2
Win? They're not even supposed to
keep score. Don't you know anything?
It's all about "playing the game",
not winning. That way everybody
wins.

                SALESMAN 1
C'mon. Don't the kids keep track of the
score anyway

                SALESMAN 2
Of course they do. But the "you have
to be fair" types are always there
to remind the children that
competition is bad.

                SALESMAN 1
Poor kids. Real life
is gonna be a big surprise.

They walk by a glass conference room.
Sitting in the room
around a big table are three people. BOB
SIMON, 50's, sits

across from two very stern looking MEN. Bob appears to be talking.

The Salesmen slow down and look. Salesman 1 chuckles and points at Bob.

> SALESMAN 1 (CONT'D)
> I know exactly what Bob's saying right now.

> SALESMAN 2
> Yeah? What?

Salesman 1 changes his posture and slumps a little.

> SALESMAN 1
> "I'm sorry. My fault. I'll take the blame. Just tell me you still like me. Tell me you love me."

They both laugh and walk down the hall.

INT. OFFICE - CONFERENCE ROOM -- DAY

Bob leans over the table to the Men.

> BOB
> Again, I'm really sorry. I take the blame for this.

INT. OFFICE - BOB'S CUBICLE -- DAY

Bob types on his computer. Salesman 1 sticks his head over

the cubicle wall.

                    SALESMAN 1
Hey. You get out of there unscathed?

Bob looks up.

                    BOB
I hope so. I couldn't save the deal
with Allied and they were counting
on it.

                    SALESMAN 1
I saw how that came down. Mission
beat our price. Simple as that.
Those guys know it.

                    BOB
Nah. I screwed it up somehow.

Bob's phone rings and he picks it up.

                    BOB
This is Bob.

Salesman 1 walks away shaking his head.

Now, I can move on to the meat of the story, where Bob
starts his journey to healing all the problems that got him to
the permanently defeated state he's in. To introduce
secondary characters that will spur on this journey. three of
the people who will propel Bob's story.

EXT. DOWNTOWN STREET -- NIGHT

Down the street walks Bob, head down,
newspaper under his

arm. His cell rings. He answers it.

                    BOB
This is Bob.

He listens a second.

                    BOB
Call me Bob. I hate Mr. Simon,
Well yes, you're right, Mr. Simon
is better than "Simple." Wait a
minute. Who is this?

A moment.

                    BOB
Oh yeah. You're the new one, what?
No. I'm not signing anything, no
way.

A Homeless Man, TOM KELLY, 50's,
approaches Bob, his hand
out. Bob waves him off. He's back into
the cell.

                    BOB
Look, she's still my wife and I
still love her. This is fixable,
What do you mean, or else?

A moment of listening.

                    BOB
Did I tell you what happened to the
last divorce attorney that
threatened me? He was electrocuted.

Tom follows, listening in. Bob continues
with the call.

>   BOB
> Well, no. I didn't have anything
> to do with it, but the next time
> you put a basketball hoop up on
> your garage I hope you don't notice
> the power lines either.

Tom continues to follow Bob down the
street.

>   BOB
> I told you. I'm not signing
> anything until I talk directly to
> her. Tell her I'm going to St. Luke's
> Hospital later. She can meet me
> there. Or at my motel.

Bob turns a corner. Tom follows. Bob
sees this and waves him
away again.

>   BOB
> Go away.

Bob listens to the cell.

>   BOB
> No. No, I wasn't talking to you,
> but yeah, you know, that works for
> you too.

Bob ends the call. Tom moves in front of
him, cutting him
off, his hand out.

                TOM
Lawyers and ex-wives. Damn
nuisance, huh? Be easier to just
kill 'em.

                BOB
What?

                TOM
Hey, you got any money? I'm
starving here. Help a guy out, ok?

Bob stops and looks the man over. His
eyes get wide.

                BOB
Tom? Tom Kelly?

Tom looks Bob over.

                TOM
Yeah. You look familiar too.

His eyes light up.

                TOM
I knew I knew you from someplace.

He points at Bob.

                TOM
Simple Simon.

                BOB
Jesus.

Bob looks up to the sky.

>   BOB
> What did I do?

Tom puts his dirty hand on Bob's shoulder.

>   TOM
> It's old home week. Can you spare
> some cash for an old friend? You
> look like you're doing ok.

Bob squirms away from him.

>   TOM
> Just ten bucks. Or twenty, maybe?

Bob stares at him.

>   BOB
> Wow. Tom. What happened to you? You
> were the big cheese in high school.

>   TOM
> Best time of my life. No
> responsibility.

He moves close to Bob.

>   TOM
> Responsibility sucks. That
> and ex-wives. You should be happy
> yours is dumping you before she
> destroys you.

                    BOB
You know, Tom, I always told anybody
who'd listen that my wife was the
only thing that kept me from living
in the gutter.

                    TOM
Hey. That's low.

                    BOB
Yeah, sorry.

                    TOM
Do you got any money or not? For an
old friend?

                    BOB
We weren't friends. In fact, I
believe it was you that pulled my--

Tom interrupts, waving his hands.

                    TOM
--That was a long time ago. Water
under the bridge. C'mon man. Help a
guy out.

Bob reaches in his pocket and pulls out
three dollars, looks
at it, and hands them to Tom.

                    BOB
Three bucks. This is all I got.

Tom looks at the cash, then pockets it.

                    TOM

She probably left you 'cause you're
a cheap son of a bitch. Thanks for
nothing, Dickhead.

He walks away. Bob yells after him.

        BOB
It wasn't because I'm cheap.

Tom ignores him. Bob turns and walks
off.

EXT. SMALL DOWNTOWN BAR -- NIGHT

It looks like any other small bar. Some
old Christmas lights
hang around the door. The sound of live
music comes through
the open door.

Bob swings into the bar without
hesitation.

INT. SMALL DOWNTOWN BAR -- NIGHT

Music is louder as Bob plops himself on
a
barstool at the old wooden bar. The
bartender, GAIL,
30's, walks up to him with a smile.

        GAIL
Hey, Bob.

She looks up at the clock on the wall.
It reads 6:15.

                    GAIL
Little early tonight.

                    BOB
Hi Gail. Yeah, family emergency to
get to later. Could I get a beer?

                    GAIL
Comin' up. Everything ok?

                    BOB
Nothing big. Medical thing with a
relative.

Gail looks at him in puzzlement for a
second then grabs a
glass and draws the beer.

                    GAIL
Serious?

                    BOB
One can hope.

Gail steps back a second at his answer.

                    GAIL
I can't figure you out.

She hands him his beer.

                    GAIL
You've been coming in here for a
month and I don't really know
anything except your name, if it is
your name-

> BOB

I'd make up a better one than Bob.

> GAIL

- that you're pretty hard on
yourself-

Bob looks down at the bar.

> GAIL

- that you're a good tipper -

He looks back up and half smiles.

> BOB

At least you don't think I'm cheap.

She taps his ring finger.

> GAIL

- And that lately your wedding ring
is gone.

She smiles, winks, and waits for a
response. He shrugs.

> BOB

I'm not happy about it, but I'm
thrilled you noticed. You just
don't wanna go there. Way too much
baggage.

> GAIL

Oh c'mon.

> BOB

There's less baggage in the cargo
hold of a 747.

She smiles knowingly and nods to
herself.

>   GAIL
> Well, just a thought.

He looks down at his beer. A MAN down
the bar waves for
her attention. He takes a drink from his
beer and looks up
to where she was.

>   BOB
> I appreciate the thought-

Gail is down the bar serving the Man and
happily talking
to him.

>   BOB
> Well crap.

He takes another drink and stares into
space, eyes glassing
over.

There's a Woman's scream. Bob looks up
to see a
MASKED GUNMAN, holding a machine gun,
standing in the front doorway. Dressed
all in black, the man fires the gun,
mowing everyone in the bar down in a
bloody mess.

Gail screams, takes two quick rounds to the chest, and goes
down behind the bar. Bob watches this all without moving
from his seat. The Gunman moves further into the bar, right
by Bob, mowing down the band and everyone else in sight.

With everyone dead, the Gunman plants himself next to Bob at
the bar, gun still smoking. Bob looks around the room, then
at the Gunman. The Gunman drops his gun down on the bar and
pulls the mask off. Bob looks at him and cringes.

> BOB

Dad?

Bob's DAD, a vital 85, grabs Bob's beer.

> DAD

Hey kiddo, mind if I have the rest
of this?

Dad drinks the beer down then looks down
the bar.

> DAD

Where's that bartender? The cute
one.

He winks at Bob.

> DAD

Wouldn't mind having some of that.

                    BOB
You shot her.

                    DAD
Oh. Yeah. Well. It's ok, I know
the owner here. Justin.

He looks at Bob.

                    DAD
You seen Justin?

Bob points to a body in the corner.

                    BOB
Right there. You know, this is the
first time I've ever seen you screw
up a relationship with a restaurant
owner.

Dad looks at Justin's body, then shrugs.

                    DAD
Worth it. We needed the time
alone. We never get any.

                    BOB
What do you want?

                    DAD
Well, I want to discuss this great
investment opportunity with you.

Dad gets serious.

                    DAD
I need to borrow ten thousand
dollars. No lose situation.

Bob's mouth drops open.

                    DAD
Ok. So how much can you spare?

Bob picks the gun up off the bar and
shoots Dad right between
the eyes. Dad teeters on the barstool
for a second and falls
off it, onto the floor. Bob picks up his
beer and drinks
the last bit on the bottom, then slams
it on the counter.

                    GAIL (O.S.)
You want another one?

Startled, Bob looks up at Gail standing
in front of him. The
band plays and everyone in the bar is
happily going on with
their business.

                    BOB
Uh, no. I'd better go. My
father's in the hospital.

                    GAIL
Oh no. I'm so sorry.

                    BOB
Don't be. We're not that close. But
thanks.

Bob reaches in his pocket and has nothing. He cringes.

> BOB
> I don't believe this. I gave my cash away. I'm sorry.

> GAIL
> Go. Go. Beer's on me.

Bob smiles back.

> BOB
> Thanks Gail. I'll get you next time.

> GAIL
> Promises. Promises.

He smiles at her and pushes the stool back to leave.

This is the first ten pages of the script. The inciting incident has yet to happen, or has it? It doesn't matter. It's enough for the reader to say, "What the heck is going on, these characters are interesting, and what happens next?" and you've met three of the major players in the film, besides Bob, and know who and what they are. Gail, Tom, and Dad. And you've been given, unknown to you yet, the impetus for a lot unexpected actions and conflict in the future, the next from Gail, surprisingly, that changes Bob's life, and one set up in those 10 pages that doesn't pay off until the climax of the script, and it's not what you might think.

Yes, complex and nothing left to chance. That 6:15 time on the clock? Very important to what's coming. Lots of subtextual information that all pays off later in some very interesting ways.

Did I know exactly how when I wrote them? Not exactly. I had an idea based on the premise, but that brings me to how I write the rest of my original scripts once I have the premise, main characters, ending, and first 10 pages.

I let the characters take me on the adventure to the ending. The characters have a goal that never changes. A path they are on. To that one point where I think the reader will go "Wow", as it all comes together. Sometimes I bullet point what I think comes next for a few scenes, sometimes I don't because it's very clear to me where it's going. But then those bullet points can get jettisoned as I write when the characters say, "Nope. We're going here instead. It's better for the story." It's all fluid and I'm not afraid to go with my gut or go with what my characters tell me.

No. I don't hear voices. I pay attention. I never lose sight of overall story. Neither should you. Each scene is part of a living breathing entity, each adding to its life until the ending, where it becomes complete. I see writers string scenes together looking for a story all the time. This is because they never look at each of those scenes as integral parts of something whole. The whole they often lose sight of. And the second that happens, readers put your script down.

This is your job. If you want to be a successful screenwriter, you need to do this. Never write a line in your script without knowing how it fits and advances the story you're trying to tell. Never write a scene that can exist without the scene before or after it.

This takes knowing your story, your characters, and where they are at all times. This is story management. Every writer uses different tools to get them to this point of understanding. I keep it in my head and manage it from there. I don't encourage this for others because I know it's borderline insane to. So, until you find your path, the writing method that is best for you, you need to try different things.

I also rewrite as I write. Like I said, I don't believe in vomit drafts. I'm always adding new things as I think of them. And when you add new unexpected things to your story as you write you have to take into account the "ripple effect" on the rest of the story.

RIPPLE EFFECT

Ok, let's say you're writing your script and come to a point where it would be better if your protagonist had a sister for some reason, a new plot point that works better for the story you're telling. So you add the sister at page 44, except you now need to go back to maybe page 12 and add her to a scene so the reader knows who she is when she shows up on 44, but maybe that's not enough, you can use her to give some subtext on page 23, she's rippled back into the story. Some gurus will tell you to just keep writing and not worry about how she effects the rest of the story, fixing it at a later date in rewrites.

That's why I rewrite as I write. I'm not looking for perfection. That's not attainable anyway, but you need to fix what's fresh in your head at the time and not let that moment fade until it's hazy, or worse, completely forgotten, later.

So, once I hit the last lines of the script and the first draft is done, on to the rewrites. No first draft of any script is ready to be seen. That's my method. Your own writing method can only come with practice and experimentation. You can't be impatient. It will take time to find.

CHAPTER 8

WRITING TO BUDGET

Movies and TV series have finite costs to produce built into them. They have budgets. The money producers want to spend on it. Sometimes the number is set the way it is because that's all the money they have to spend on it. There isn't any more. Writers need to be aware of these numbers.

This is one subject that really gets some people in a lather. Should you pay attention to the budget of the script you're writing? Or, should you just write the story you want to write and to hell with how much it will cost to make?

I've had writers tell me that it's ridiculous for screenwriters to worry about such things. That if producers love their script, they'll get the money to make it, or cut it down to fit the budget they need. This kind of thinking is not only shortsighted, it's completely wrong.

Every writer who starts a script should have a figure in mind of how much the film or show will cost before they write it, because it will affect your creative choices. It will make you more creative, if you do it correctly.

And if you don't think producers won't flat out ask you "What's the budget?", you don't know this business.

Why? Because they won't read scripts out of their budget range, no matter how good you think it is. They know what's a realistic money figure for them and know they aren't going over it. So, you'd better have an answer for them that fits into the budget ranges and terms the industry uses.

Films fall into four classifications in terms of money spent on them. The industry actually uses the word "budget" in these terms. Let's define what these terms mean in dollars.

Ultra-Low Budget Films: Under $1.2 million

Low Budget Films: $1.2 to $ 5 million

Mid-range Films: $5 to $475 million

High Budget: $75 to $250 million

WHAT BUDGET SHOULD A NEW WRITER WRITE?

Every new writer has their huge sci-fi script or fantasy ala *Lord of the Rings* or *Game of Thrones* or action adventure the size of *Fast and Furious*. Their studio film. Heck, I have a couple of those. Neither one, however, was my first script. If it had been, I would have learned what I'm going to tell you now. You can't sell a big budget script as a new writer. Hey, right now, established writers can't sell one.

Why not?

First, there isn't anyone to buy them. Only a small handful of places have the money or structure in place to make them. These would be the studios or well-financed A-list production companies and mini-majors, and they aren't buying many new spec scripts. Especially from new writers.

But what about the streaming services? I've seen budgets like that on some of their films. Yes, you have. Very few, and all, every single one, from established writers or writer/directors. The streaming services aren't interested in any writer they haven't heard of for their big budget stuff. This, I've heard directly from producers' mouths. If you have a track record of success, the door might be open. Otherwise, not so much.

If you're writing your big budget script as a future writing sample, using it to try to get a big budget writing job somewhere down the line, I get it. It doesn't hurt to have a couple in your stack of spec scripts. They're fun to write.

To expect to sell big budget scripts or get any work out of them as a new writer is a whole different matter. Producers won't even read them because they can't make them. And studios don't read them because they're too busy making franchise films, sequels to those franchises, films based on characters from those franchises, or films based on million selling novels, or a comic book, or a cancelled TV show, or a video game, or an iconic cartoon, or an amusement park ride, or a board game, before they'll make a big budget spec. They'll remake a previously failed film before they'll make a big budget spec. This is the way it is. They make these decisions based on their business models, not by what you want them to do.

Now, before you fill my inbox with all the exceptions, I am aware of them and also know I can count those on one hand in the last five years. And films by iconic directors don't count. Plus, those big budget exceptions weren't new writers either. All were from established writers in the industry. You don't have to be paying much attention to see this trend and that it isn't going to change. Add unproduced writer to your resume and the odds of being one of these exceptions go down to absolute zero.

What about Mid-Range, Bob? I have a 30-million-dollar film that kicks butt, well, sorry, nobody is making mid-range films. It's a graveyard for Mid-Range films out there. Well, there is one company that has been trying, but it's been a struggle. You have to show a huge return to make any money. And they've only bought from established producers and writers 99% of the time.

So, what does the smart new writer do? My advice?

As a new writer trying to break in, if you write your scripts, or most of your scripts, with a budget of a million to five million dollars, some maybe even less. There are tons of producers and production companies that want to read what you have, and they can actually buy them and make them. In these cases, they don't care if you're new or not. In this budget range, if they read a script they love, it doesn't matter.

So again, I'll do the math. Who can make your scripts if they're big budget? You can count the number of places on your fingers. Versus hundreds, maybe even thousands of buyers if you write low budget. Hmmm. Basically, zero chance versus an actual chance.

Not much of a choice if you want to realistically see anything you wrote on a screen.

They don't need a lot of audience support to make money. A million-dollar film that takes in six million? Profitable. A success to finance people, and those are the people that matter in the long run. No money. No movies.

I know this is something a lot of new writers find hard to swallow. They love big budget studio films and they want more than anything to write films the studios make, to walk red carpets, to see their name on a poster and on a big screen. Believe me when I tell you that the low budget film is a quicker ticket there than writing huge budget scripts and looking for a miracle that has no chance of happening.

Where do you think the big studios get their writers? From writers who wrote low budget films that were critical or box office successes. Every one of those writers started there. You can trace it back. You won't be an exception.

Those writers wrote innovative fun or scary or thrilling scripts that were made into great low budget films. Low budget doesn't mean low quality. It means the filmmakers were able to make an entertaining film on a fixed budget of $1-$5 million.

And this doesn't mean the final budget on your film might not be higher. Many $5 million budget scripts got made for twice that much or more after attracting higher paid stars and directors, which attracted more money for bigger and better locations, effects, or stunts. But to begin with, you need to stay in that range with your written spec.

I understand your disappointment. You want to write what you want to write. They're your stories, your scripts, and truthfully, you can do whatever you want. But you also want to take advantage of the best shot at success, and writing lower budget scripts is exactly that.

You need to understand that writers who write on assignment, who are hired to write films for every kind of production company or producer, are given the parameters of their job and those parameters include the budget they have to write for. If you want to be a professional writer, you need to be able to do this.

As someone who does this kind of assignment writing, because of my business background and my understanding of what costs are in film, knowledge learned on set and by research, I get jobs where a producer will hand me a script and say, "Don't change the story or the dialogue, just take a million dollars out of the budget." And they pay me for that. If I can't do that, they can't make the film because they don't have that extra million dollars to spend.

I get hired to do rewrites on scripts, other writer's scripts, where I have to be very aware of the budget involved every time. I always ask, "What's the budget?" in the meetings so I know what to write and not write as I rewrite these scripts. It is what professional writers do every day.

I get hired to write scripts from premises that producers come up with. The first thing they tell me is what budget to write for. It's a very important part of the job.

And something you need to learn to do.

This is only about what's in the script and on screen. The story. You don't worry about fixed costs of a film that have nothing to do with what's in the script.

So, the next question you'll have is: What did you learn on set and in your research and from experience writing for productions about what things in scripts cost?

THINGS TO THINK ABOUT WRITING A LOW BUDGET FILM

1. Actors cost money. When I'm writing any low budget script, I automatically limit the number of speaking parts to 17 or less, 14 is the sweet spot. Yes, this includes all the one-line parts. The less principal characters (speaking characters) you have, the less a film costs. This is why in films when you see a character ask someone a question and the responder just points instead of saying something? Or there's a couple and only one of them says anything? That's because they're saving money by using extras instead. The cost difference is huge, especially if you're using SAG actors, which they have to be if your leads are familiar faces. If you have too many speaking parts, think about combining characters, if you can. On one script I was taking money out of, I took three characters and made them one. It worked well without effecting the story at all.

2. Extras. Big scenes with lots of extras cost money. Lots of it. Limit these if you can. I took a high school football scene and made it a basketball scene and cut the extras by three quarters. Big street scenes are expensive. Anything very public where you need a lot of people to make it look real.

3. Locations. Limit your locations. Use as few as you can, and use as many of those locations as you can over and over. Every time you have a new location, they have to move all the equipment and trucks. This costs a lot of money. The fewer locations you use, the less money spent. If your characters eat out a lot, make it the same restaurant. Also, the bigger the location the more it costs. Stadiums. Downtown in big cities. International locations. Supermarkets.

Malls. Airports. You get the idea. Smaller locations = less money. This doesn't affect story, just where the story takes place. You have to be creative.

4. Indoor versus Outdoor Locations. Indoor is cheaper by a lot. You don't have to worry about all the things you have no control over outdoors when you're indoors and those things can slow down production, which costs you money. So, anything indoor is going to cost less and be more efficient. The more control over the environment you have, the better for the budget.

5. Weather. Weather? Yep, rain, snow, tornadoes, all expensive. Yes, some can be done VFX, but unless you have the budget to do it right, you've seen how that looks. Unless some specific weather plays a plot point in your film, leave it out. That includes sunsets and sunrises.

6. Day versus Night. It costs a lot more to shoot a night scene than it does a day scene. Indoor night scenes can be controlled by lighting. It's outdoor night scenes that cost a lot more. Unless it's crucial to the plot and your story timeline to shoot at night, make them day scenes. One film I worked on, I was able to take more than a dozen night scenes and make them day scenes, again without effecting the story at all. The original writer wasn't thinking budget, which might have helped that writer stay on the project longer instead of being replaced by me.

7. Moving Vehicles. Shooting any scene inside a moving vehicle costs more money. In setups. In equipment costs. In time it takes to shoot them. All of these things equal extra money spent. Shooting in anything that's moving is expensive. This doesn't mean you can't have them in your script. I've put a few in my own low budget scripts. Just make them count and keep the number down. I have people talk

outside the car before getting in or inside a parked car if I can. If you have to do it, make sure it's plot driven.

8. Explosions and Gunfire. Expensive. They require a lot of time setting up, extra crew to handle them, stunt people, EFX people, armorers, and a lot of time to shoot. Again, doesn't mean you can't have them in your low budget script. Make them count. Huge lengthy gun fights are mostly cost prohibitive. Huge explosions, also, but a couple, written right, can be done. I had two explosions in *Extracurricular Activities* and we were able to do it with an under $5 million budget.

9. Car Chases. These can't be done well with a low budget. They eat up shooting days and lots of money. You have to shut down streets. Stunt drivers. Special cars. They have to be practiced and choreographed. It's a logistical nightmare for a low budget film. Leave them out if you can. If you need one, make it easy to film, like on a deserted country road. Same for car wrecks. Incredibly expensive. Think of other ways to get what you want from the plot, if you can.

10. Stunts. You need to hire stunt people. Stunt coordinators. Expensive. Take a lot of time to shoot, so they consume shoot days. Any big set piece that uses stunts can be a budget killer. Be careful with these. Again, one or two might work. No more than that. I think you're getting the idea that any action is expensive. You can do it, but you have to be careful and creative.

11. EFX & CGI. These things are getting cheaper and cheaper every day, but you still have to be careful how you use them. You can write action you know is going to be CGI, but understand it needs to be in locations where there's control over the environment

to save money. CGI monsters still cost, so reveal them as late as you can in the story. Be smart.

12. Period Films. Any story that doesn't take place NOW is more expensive. Setting something in the Old West or Elizabethan times, anything before technology, is better. There are loads of costumes available and horses and sets. Still expensive. But you get into the 20's thru the 90's? You have no idea how expensive. You have to have period cars, sets, costumes, hairstyles, the list goes on and on; all the tech from those eras. Producers of low budget films hate period pieces because of the expense.

13. Animals. Trainers. The animals cost a lot. They take time. Extra shooting days. You can have animals, but understand, the more exotic the animal, the more it costs.

14. Kids. They require on set teachers. They can only work certain hours. You can absolutely write them into your script, or have kid-based films, but know it's an extra expense as you write your script and cut elsewhere.

This is a very rudimentary list, but it gives you an idea. I know looking at it you're thinking, "What can I write then?"

You can write a lot. More than you think. Go watch some contemporary low budget films and see what they did. Read scripts from low budget films and look how they wrote it. If you're smart and do things sparingly, you can have a parade or a shootout on a street or a foot chase or blow up something small, Anything is doable if you are creative and understand you need to have a bunch of cheaper scenes leading up to these things. You don't have to sacrifice story. But you also have to choose a premise that fits a lower budget.

One to $5 million is still a lot of money. You can use it to tell a good story and have a few of the things that cost. In *Extracurricular Activities*, I ran a Humvee off a cliff and exploded it, all CGI. I blew up a parked Corvette. I had one gun shoot one bullet. I had one stunt where someone got hit by that bullet. And had multiple deaths, most of them off screen. The ones on screen were simple and you never saw the bodies afterward. I did have some shots in moving cars. Not many, but they had to be there. I had one rainstorm, completely plot driven. I had one high school Basketball game with a bunch of extras. Had a high school kegger party at night, outdoors, with one underwater shot. And so on. It worked for the film. It all looks great. Under $5 million. But these scenes were a small part of an overall story, and it didn't require as much money to shoot the rest of it.

You can do most anything with a lot of thought. You just can't overdo it.

This is all to help you understand that screenwriters start at the bottom, like any other business you want to get into. You start in the equivalent of the mailroom. And that's what low budget scripts are. Your mailroom time is there so you can use it to get promotions to the next level. Every successful writer has done this. Low budget scripts are your entre to doing this for a living. Producers know if you can do this, you can do anything.

You also need to understand budget so you can get and keep the assignment work that make up the majority of screenwriting jobs. There are many factors that make this a must for any screenwriter to learn and use.

CHAPTER 9

REWRITES/OWNERSHIP/FEEDBACK

Once you have finished your script, you put it away for a week or two. Get your eyes and brain off of it. By this time, and after working on it for so many hours, you're too familiar with it to see it objectively anymore, so a little vacation from it is in order.

When I feel I've spent enough time away, I print the script out. Yes, three-hole punch paper. Yes, I put brads in the two edge holes. Just like the good old days when this was how you sent out your scripts. You can choose not to do this and make your notes from reading it on your computer or iPad. But either way, you need to make notes. Lots of them.

Me? I'm a printed out copy of the script kinda guy. So, with red and blue pens in my hand, I read every single word in the script, finding all kinds of bad stuff I didn't see before. Scenes that don't work. Scenes that are missing. Scenes that are out of order for the story to work. Dialogue that doesn't work. Characters that need more work. Set ups that need to be set up better. Payoffs that aren't. Twists that need more clues. Twists that don't work. Twists I discover.

Lots of things crossed out in red. Lots of notes on the edge of the pages in blue.

One thing you need to understand. Nothing in your script should be sacred. You have to be of the mindset that there's nothing in your script that can't be deleted, changed, or replaced. If you make your mind up that this is the case, it's easier to be open to making your work much better. Truth is, things you take out now are things you might put back on the next rewrite. Not necessarily in the same place in the script either.

You need to learn now, editing yourself, that anything can change in a script so the shock of it when you get producer notes in the future isn't fatal to your career.

So, what do you look for and do?

First and foremost, everything you read should be looked at in terms of your overall story. That needs to be on your mind at all times. With that in your mind:

You shorten action sequences that need it. Fix those that are unclear. Add to the action with new ideas that you'll get from being fresh with it.

Go through each scene thinking, "In late. Out early".

Check all your dialogue. Every word. See what you need to restate or reword. See what you need to cut. See what you need to add for clarity or maybe something new that works better. Or maybe a character that's not in a scene now needs to be there, or cut out. Find new ways to say things with more subtext.

This is also where you red pen those extra sentences in your dialogue that restate what's already been said earlier. Where you get rid of exposition, even if it's subtext that you've already given the reader before and restated for emphasis.

Here's a really good rule of thumb: if you've told an audience something they need to know, you don't need to do it again and again just to make sure they get it. This happens all the time in first drafts because, it just does. Now it's time to get rid of them.

Readers, producers, and audiences are smart. Readers want to read your script looking for something that will make them a hero with producers. Producers want something that will make them look good and make them money. Audiences? They've either paid to see your film or chosen to watch it. Your script is probably less than a hundred pages. Readers and producers can keep track of things that long. You don't need to hit them over the head with your plot points every five pages. Audiences can pay attention, if they're interested, for 90 minutes.

You've watched films that did this and hated it, because the writer or director thought you weren't smart enough to get what they were trying to tell you, so they told you over and over?

I watched a film like this not long ago. Not good. I actually got angry because of the waste of good storytelling time used to reiterate things as much as they could, so that when their big moment came, they expected you to go, "Oh, wow!"

When the big moment came in this film, I looked at my wife and rolled my eyes because I knew it was coming. And it wasn't good. If they had respected the audience, it would've had a much bigger impact. Trust your audience. Trust the reader and the producer. You don't have to say anything more than once if you say it right.

So, get rid of the redundancies. You will find them.

Once you're done marking up your paper script, or from your computer:

You have all your notes. Your changes and deletions. Time to implement them.

Make a copy of your original script and paste it into a new file in your screenwriting software. Never ever overwrite the original script. Always keep a copy of every version of what you write.

Name the file for each rewrite in numerical order. *MyScriptv1, MyScriptv2*, and so on. It's very important for them to be orderly because you never know when you'll need something from a different version. This happens all the time. Including after you've sold it and get notes. Sometimes those notes are for something you already had in an earlier version of the script that you can go back and retrieve because you saved it. This has happened to me more than once. Part of the job.

I always use the last version I wrote as a template when rewriting. Some writers like to start from scratch with a blank page. You have to do what works for you. I love having a template of the story there, even if I'm going to eviscerate it.

You also can't be afraid to ask yourself the "What if?" question about your own script rewrites. What if I change the protagonist from male to female? What if instead of having my protagonist be a veterinarian, or they work in a tire store? What if, What if. Don't be afraid of change that might make your script much better.

You change what you have to. You keep what you have to. You work to make it better.

What you don't want is a script you can't make better because it's not right to begin with. This is the worst.

That's why, as I've said about rewriting and nothing being sacred, sometimes while you're writing your first draft you have to be honest and realize it's not working when it's not, and make the radical changes it needs right then so it can work.

BACKTRACKING

Some history,

A few years ago, sometime in the fall when I was in LA, I was lucky enough to find myself sitting across a conference table from the head of a pretty big production company. His development exec had brought me in to pitch a couple of things she liked. In the room were the development exec, a sofa full of interns, the head of the production company, his assistant, and a well-known actress that came with me because, well, it made sense since one of the pitches was written with her in mind and she's a good friend, so it couldn't hurt. Plus, she's great to hang with. They weren't unhappy she came with me.

After some introductions, mostly the interns, and some idle chatter, I got down to business and pitched the movie idea I had with this actress in mind. I got about a minute into it and the boss turned to his assistant and said, "We're buying this, let the business office know."

Yes, my jaw dropped. The actress's jaw dropped. Afterward, she said she'd never seen this happen in 25 years in the business. But there it was. They also asked for a synopsis they could approve before I started writing. At that point I probably would have agreed to anything, because shock.

So, I went home and wrote one. Did I like it? Absolutely. To me, it worked. It worked for them, too. They said, "Get going on it." I got a contract, signed it after a little negotiation, and started on the script.

I was really happy with the first 10 pages. It flowed. My female protagonist was sharply drawn, I thought. So far, the supporting characters worked well, too. I had an ending that worked for what I wanted to do based on the synopsis and my bullet points.

But, and this is a big but, when I got to my male protagonist on page thirteen and began to work on the meat of the story with the both of them, I hated him and what was happening to the story. A story I thought I had well planned out. A story the production company approved. But this guy? This character? He was a nothing burger. The two protagonists had zero chemistry. My fault, because I set him up to fail in the synopsis but didn't realize it.

And yet, I wrote on and was painting myself into a story corner because this guy was so lame. Dilemma? You bet. The deadline clock was running, and they approved this storyline based on my premise which I still believed was rock solid, so I forced myself forward. As I did this, I found it harder and harder to motivate myself to write. The lure of the internet, playing with Rocket the Dog, little chores around the house, screeners to watch. Anything but writing. Guilt? You bet. Admitting I was wrong? Not yet.

I had to force myself to open the file. To waste more time, I decided to reread what I'd written so far. And there, on page 7, it was. My "what if" moment. A three-line minor character I put there to help establish a location, greeted me waving his arms wildly and yelling, "Look at me!! What about me?!" And I said, "What if this guy was the male protagonist?"

I sat, my brain finally fully engaged in this writing process I'd been avoiding, and thought about the possibilities. And like a beautiful lightning strike, the whole story opened up. A new much more meaningful emotional ending. A way to build this relationship surprisingly and with intelligence. The whole thing. It was all there. *Zowie.*

It also meant deleting 42 pages of script completely. Gone. Deleting 42 pages of hard struggle. Of hours and hours of work. And now I had completely new story points to work out.

Took me about 30 seconds to think about it and do it. I hit the delete key. Don't worry, I still had a backup.

Victory was mine. Then I thought, "Uh oh."

I needed to make the call to the producer and explain I was keeping the premise, the basic plot, but was completely changing direction in the story and would they please let me. She was totally receptive as I explained exactly where the story now needed to go to work well. She asked a couple of excellent questions as she always does, and then said, "I like it. Go and do it."

I know it's unfathomable to realize that writers, no matter how much they prepare themselves, can be completely wrong about their story after they're that far into it. Sarcasm aside, you as a writer owe it to yourself, your characters, your story, to listen to that little voice that says "This is not working" when it happens instead of plowing ahead thinking you can write your way out of it, with a first draft that's 100% wrong. A first draft that's rewritable at all, unless you kill it completely.

You're much better off killing it earlier in the game and fixing it now. The delete key is your friend. "What if" is your friend. Don't fear using them liberally if you have to.

This isn't the first time this has happened to me, but never on this big a level or these circumstances. I find new stuff and get new ideas while writing, not just from me but from my characters, so I constantly go back and adjust. This time it was major. But after my "Aha" moment I didn't hesitate because you have to service your story before your ego. If I had kept going with my original storyline, the script wouldn't have worked. And any rewrites would be based on a script that didn't work. Plus, I'm not going to turn in a script that doesn't work. Neither should you.

Among all the other stuff you have to do as a screenwriter is to question the honesty of your work as you go along. Be truthful with yourself. It's not easy and it hurts a lot sometimes. But it also makes the big picture of what you're trying to do better, healthier.

If you see a character obviously not working, stop and fix it, even if it means radical change. Relationships in the story or conflict not working? Stop. If you force these things forward when they obviously don't work it kills good story and killing good story kills scripts, essentially completely wasting your time on your project.

Don't make the mistake of having a script you can't rewrite to improve because it's already a lost cause. And believe me, scripts can be lost causes.

FEEDBACK

One of the most important things you can do after your first or second rewrite is to get feedback on your script.

This doesn't include getting feedback from your family or your friends who have never read a screenplay. They are always going to love it and give you, a lot of the time, false positive feedback. You will hear what you always wanted to hear about your work, so there's that. But it's not of any real benefit.

What you want to do is find people who know the format and don't really know you to read your script. Then, most of the time, you'll get real feedback. Not all of it is going to be good.

Ok, Bob. So, as a writer in, well, Anytown USA, how do I find these writers?

Not easy, but doable. In many larger towns, and many smaller ones, there are screenwriting groups that meet monthly or bi-monthly. Find one of those if you can and join in. I know here where I live there are about 30 of them and I'm not in LA.

They aren't always a good fit for everyone, and a lot of bad advice and misinformation gets passed along at these meet-ups. Mostly about the non-existent rules and how if you break them, you'll be blackballed by the Hollywood Moguls. Don't argue with these people no matter how wrong they are, what you want to get out of these meetings is people you can share your scripts with.

This means you'll have to read their scripts and give them feedback, too. It's not a one-way street.

You'll run into the full gamut of reactions to your feedback, from genuine thanks and open minds to people who might cry.

An example:

A friend asked me to read a script for the son of his friend. I did, because this was a friend, I've known for 40+ years and you do that for friends.

One-hundred-two pages. The premise was pretty good. A solid idea. The execution of the premise? Oh boy. Mostly not there at all with some passable hints of ok, here and there. Spelling was atrocious. Dialogue nobody on this planet would say, ever. A lot of exposition. The worst kind of exposition. People telling people things they would already know to inform the audience. For a first script it was a pretty standard try.

We spoke on the phone. I told the writer the truth, in my eyes, about what was wrong with the script. I started by telling the writer how good I thought the idea was. How I wish I'd thought of it. Then I started in, I think gently, to tell the writer how off the mark the script was in a lot of fixable ways and why. I didn't get very far when the writer interrupted and said, "You're hurting my feelings. Why are you so mean?" I'm not kidding. I may have laughed for a split second. "Seriously?" I said.

"Yes."

I was flummoxed. I've gotten a lot of reaction to feedback, never this one.

He went on to explain that all his friends and family thought the script was great and would be a wonderful film. All he had to do was get it to an agent or studio and let nature take the course he wanted it to. Why was I being so mean? Why couldn't I just read it and pass it on to those people. Or not read it and pass it on. This was his honest thought process.

I said, "Is this a joke?" I was trying to think of which writer friend of mine would have put him up to this and how I was going to get them back.

He assured me it wasn't a joke and I said, "You know, I went easy on you. A reader would have just thrown your script in the trash on about page three and never said anything to try and help you. A producer wouldn't have been that nice. This is a tough business and you have to be tough too."

I told him that he'd have to measure up to industry standards or be left behind and that meant listening to honest constructive criticism and leaving his feelings at the door. That criticism of his work wasn't personal, and he shouldn't take it that way. He honestly didn't understand. You could hear it in his voice.

I told him I wasn't sending it anywhere. I told him if he sent it out, he was going to hear a lot worse than what I said or nothing at all. I told him I was going to delete his script from my computer, and I would take my mean old self as far away from him as I could.

I was given a tremendous amount of help and advice when I was first starting. Help from some amazing pros who didn't have to, especially considering where my stupid ego was after selling my first script out of the box. But they did. And I listened and I learned, and I made mistakes and I fixed my mistakes. Because I had that kind of help.

Honest help that wasn't what I wanted to hear most of the time.

There's that kind of help out there for you if you're open to it. Help that makes your scripts better.

I have a circle of about two dozen amazing professional writers and producers and directors out there who read my new spec scripts, and I read theirs. How did I find them?

Some, I found on Twitter. There's not a special section or anything, but you look up the screenwriters you like and follow them. Those professionals will not be reading your scripts, so don't ask. There will be writers like you, following these same professionals. Start communicating with them. Build friendships. I've met the best writers who've given me the best feedback that way.

There are tons of screenwriting boards on Facebook. You just have to weed out the real writers from the cranks. It is the internet. Get to know people and find other writers who will give you honest feedback.

This all takes time and effort. But everything in screenwriting takes time and effort. Becoming proficient at any artform takes time and effort.

PAID FEEDBACK

Ok, this one is tough. I truly believe you can find people to give you feedback without having to pay for it. There are literally hundreds of sites out there that will take your money to give you feedback on your script. Ranging from people who have never set foot in a real production meeting and have written two short films that were made for nothing to very experienced ex-studio development people. It runs the whole gamut.

It's up to you to do your homework and find out who these people really are and if they have the qualifications to take your money and give you real feedback.

You get to ask them questions. If they don't answer them to your satisfaction, don't use them. Look them up on the Internet. They'll be there. If they aren't, run away.

But, in my opinion, a lot of these sites exist on repeat business and word of mouth. So, the question is, will you get honest hard feedback or watered-down feedback meant to keep you coming back and spending more money? I don't know. But it is something to think about.

Remember: No matter how you go out and get feedback, leave your ego and feelings at the door. Tough to do, but every writer I know that's successful does it. Why? Because you'll learn something. You'll get better as a writer. But mostly because if you don't, you won't survive in the very tough world of screenwriting.

CHAPTER 10

MARKETING YOUR SCRIPT, part one

Marketing your script is a Catch 22 (look it up). In order for your scripts to be read you have to be a successful screenwriter, but in order to become a successful screenwriter you need for your scripts to be read.

Now that you've read that a few times and are digesting it and feeling a little sick, all is not lost. You can succeed, it just takes that time and effort I keep hammering you with.

Before I get into the nuts and bolts and ideas and strategies of marketing your script out there to get it read, optioned, sold, and produced, or to just have it be a great sample of what you can do, there's a lesson you need to sit through.

THE MYTH OF INSTANT GRATIFICATION

One of the most frustrating things about screenwriting is the time it takes for anything to happen. Anything. It takes time to figure out what to write. It takes time to research it. It takes time to write it, always longer than you think to do it well. Then come your rewrites. Time. More rewrites. More time. Getting peer feedback. More time. More rewrites. More time.

Now you want someone to read it who can make it, or who can get it to someone who can make it.

Here's where we get to the most frustrating thing about dealing with new writers. Many expect instant gratification. To write their script and immediately see action on it. They have no idea about the reality of film and TV production. They think their script is so good that their thought is: I will write this script. It will sell. I will be on the red carpet at the premiere in six months.

Sounds like an exaggeration, right? It's not. I've heard it more than once. Writers are done with their script and they want it read right now. Except that's not the way it works.

Even when they do get read requests, I can't tell you how many times I've heard writers complain they haven't heard anything back from a producer or rep and it's been a whole week. Or the manager who requested it hasn't gotten back to them in a month. Or the producer who asked for it never got back to them.

Or the biggest complaint, why can't they get anyone to read their script at all? Why is it so unfair that you can't send an unsolicited script to anyone you want and have them read it the next day?

The system of submitting scripts is set up the way it is so that producers, production companies, agents, and managers are not so overwhelmed with product that they can't read anything. There are hundreds of thousands of scripts out there looking for a home. And every writer of each of these believes they have the next hit film, if only the powers that be would read them.

That includes me. Hey, you should believe in your work. It's essential to success.

The industry is set up to weed out the bad scripts before they can get to them. Thus, all the checks and balances and brick walls put up by the people in the film and TV business. It's self-protection from the avalanche of horrible scripts that would engulf them.

So, getting through those checks and balances and brick walls takes a whole lot of time and effort on your part.

Want to know how long? It's not weeks or months. You need to start thinking years. Every successful writer has endured this, and they succeeded by not giving up.

There is no instant gratification. There are no overnight successes. Every success story spent a lot of time becoming that overnight success. Knowing this, and after you have registered your copyright and you think your script is ready to be seen by producers or agents or managers, you have to market the heck out of it.

Ok Bob, how do I get my script read? Glad you asked…

THE QUERY LETTER

New writers can't send their scripts to producers and reps. They won't accept them, read them, or consider them. Period. No one has an open submission policy. There used to be a couple, but they were so flooded with scripts that it ground their businesses to a halt. They were buried in hundreds of thousands of scripts. They stopped having that policy.

The reasons are many for not just letting you send your script, mostly the sheer number of scripts, but also the mountain of legal ramifications they face if they were to do this.

You can be upset or think it's not fair, I've heard it all. They don't care if it's not fair to you. It works for them. They're businesses and they get to operate their businesses as they see fit. Some producers, production companies, agents, and managers have given new writers avenues to get to them. They're very twisty avenues, but they are there.

Notice I left off the studios and the streaming services from the list that will give you the opportunity to get your script to them. They don't want to see your script unless an agent, manager, producer they know, or production company they know, brings it to them. This is something that will never change, so don't think you'll be special and get your script to them. You won't. For the rest of them, you need a query letter.

Ok. What's a query letter, Bob?

A short sweet email, sent to producers or managers or agents or production companies that accept them, to ask them nicely if they'd like to read your script.

What's in a query letter?

The title of your script should be in the subject line. That's it. Don't use the word "query" in the subject line in case they send any email to spam with that word in the subject line. Sadly, that's a real thing at some of these companies.

The body of the letter needs to be personal to the person you're sending it to.

```
Producer or Rep Name Here,
```

To Whom It May Concern is a bad thing. They know it's just one in the few hundred you sent, but if you want them to pay attention to you, you pay attention to them.

Note: You can send a few hundred at the same time, just make each one personal to the person you're sending it to.

Next is an introduction of who you are. It's not a bio. It's not about you telling them anything other than your name. Short, sweet.

```
I'm Bob / Bobette Screenwriter and I've
written a thriller called "Thriller" and
looking at what you have produced in the
past, I think it would be a good fit.
```

Note: If you're going to say this, then actually look at what they have done in the past, so you don't look ridiculous when all they've produced is Christmas movies. Do your homework.

Next, you place in the query letter your carefully crafted LOGLINE.

What's a logline? It's a one or two sentence description, 25 to 50 words, of the overall idea of the story. It's the story that you want to convey to your audience.

A good way to explain it is, when your friends ask you what a movie you saw was about, how you'd describe it in a sentence or two.

This is the logline from *Church People*, a script I worked on.

```
A    youth    pastor    questions    the
commercialization    of    his    church's
ministry,    his    personal    relationships,
how    to    truly    affect    the    lives    of    the
kids    he    ministers    to,    and    how    to    keep
from    being    crucified    by    his    head    pastor
in    the    next    Easter    Passion    play.
```

It's 42 words long, so you don't have to count them. Wait. What? I've been told that if your logline is more than 25 words long, they won't read it and they might come to your house and kill your dog.

You've been told wrong. Do you really think producers and reps count the words in a logline? They don't count the words. Twenty-five words is great, if you can describe your film well in that many words, but you get to go over 25 if that's what it takes. Some films can't be loglined in 25 words and get the interest needed to be read. No one cares. As long as their interest is piqued.

By the way, *Church People* got bought and made.

How about another one? Here's the logline from *Extracurricular Activities*:

```
A    model    high    school    junior    sets    the
curves    in    all    his    classes    and    has    an
```

afterschool job killing parents for his classmates, frustrating a local cop who knows, but can't prove it.

Thirty-two words. Producers lined up to read this script. It was optioned 8 different times by 8 different producers, production companies, and one studio before it got made. They just want to read something that interests them. They don't count the words.

Here's one you'll recognize.

PIRATES OF THE CARIBBEAN: THE CURSE OF THE BLACK PEARL

Blacksmith Will Turner teams up with eccentric pirate "Captain" Jack Sparrow to save his love, the governor's daughter, from Jack's former pirate allies, who are now undead.

Twenty-seven words, Wait. What? They used names. I thought they weren't supposed use names or they reject it? Nope. Nobody cares. And if I read this logline without knowing anything about it, I'd want to read the script.

If you think you need it, there's very a rudimentary template to help writers with their loglines:

When **(INCITING INCIDENT)** happens, **(THE PROTAGONIST)** decides **(THIS ACTION)** against **(THE ANTAGONIST)**.

This gives you an idea of what's needed in a logline, but it's not set in stone. You get to play with it to get what you want.

Remember: A logline is a snapshot of your story. The whole screenplay reduced to its essence.

I personally don't write my logline until I finish the script, because I'm not sure what exactly it'll be until I'm done with the screenplay. And no one asks for it until you're done anyway.

Also: A logline is not a tagline. Aliens' tagline was:

```
In Space No One Can Hear You Scream.
```

It's an amazing line for a poster, but it's not a logline. Don't mistake one for the other.

Back to our query letter:

So now you have your subject line, introduction, logline.

All that's left is asking for the read.

```
Would love to have you take a look.
Thank you and let me know if I can send
it.
```

It's that simple. Some people who advise on loglines say it's ok to use a comparison before you ask for the read. I've used them in the past. My most successful one?

```
Nancy Drew meets Stephen King and Monty
Python.
```

You can use these kinds of comparisons, but you also have to be careful because you never know if the person reading hated any of the films you use. Plus, you'd better deliver on that promise. I use them only when I know it works.

Don't do them if they look ridiculous or they're going to make people roll their eyes.

Pulp Fiction meets *My Little Pony*

Now you know what to do, so:

Here's your whole query letter.

Producer name,

Thank you for your time. I'm (Your Name Here), and I've written a black comedy thriller called *Extracurricular Activities* that I think is right in your wheelhouse. ← say your own way

A model high school junior sets the curves in all his classes and has an afterschool job killing parents for his classmates, frustrating a local cop who knows, but can't prove it.

It's *Ferris Bueller* meets *Heathers*.

Would love to have you read it. Thank you and let me know if I can send it.

Best,

Your Name here.

Simple. To the point. Doesn't take long to read. It's not cluttered. It's professional.

There *are* things you absolutely shouldn't write in a query letter.

Some Do Nots:

Do not say things like, "It's your next Oscar winning film," or "It's simply the best script you will ever read," or "This script will make you a hero in Hollywood." You get the drift. This is a business letter, treat it like a business letter. And don't make promises that are impossible to keep. These people have heard it all and hate stuff like this.

Don't call your screenplay an "award-winning" script unless it actually won an award they would have heard of. And by won, I mean won, quarterfinals, semi-finals? Those don't count as a win and it's a sure way to have them not want to work with you because you don't know the meaning of award winning.

Clue: 98% of the contests out there? Producers and reps have no idea those exist and could care less about them. You're not going to impress them and may hurt your chances of being read.

Don't write a book. If they see the letter has big blocks of text, they will delete it without reading it. Doubt me on this? Send a bunch of queries like that and see how many read requests you get.

Now, your query letter is written. What do you do next?

You heard online you need an agent or a manager to make everything easier, and you think, "I'll do that."

AGENTS AND MANAGERS

I need to get this fact out as quick as I can, so you understand it. Agents and managers are looking for writers who will have careers, not one trick ponies. You aren't going to get one from your first script unless it's so ground shatteringly good that people read it and faint from ecstasy. This is not likely. In fact, let's be honest, this isn't going to happen. It might not happen for your first ten scripts.

For sure, it is about quality, but quantity counts, too. You have to have an answer to the age-old question, "What else do you have?" besides, "Well, I got some ideas," or "Isn't this one enough?"

Four to six scripts is the sweet spot and tells them you're serious about screenwriting. And always know which one of them you want to pitch next if you get asked what else you have.

I'm also going to say there's such a thing as having too many scripts for reps and producers. If you answer the question, "What else have you got?" with, "I have 72 scripts and 37 TV pilots," they'll run away just as fast. It's not about how many you can churn out. It's about having a dozen or less that are outstanding. Some of the greatest most prolific writers out there can barely write three good original specs a year. The key word being "good". I average a little under two a year. I spend as much time preparing to write one as I do writing it. You won't impress anyone with how many scripts you can write in a year. No producer will ever ask you how fast you wrote something.

Most new writers have the wrong idea about agents and managers anyway. They think that once they have one the heavens will open and manna in the form of instant sales and produced films and writing jobs will shower over them.

A good example of this kind of thinking is from something I actually witnessed in a different aspect of this business. I was sitting in my acting agent's office one afternoon shooting the breeze and there was a commotion in the outer office. My agent, who although she's about 5'1" and pretty petite but could probably throw someone through a wall, went to see what was going on. I followed.

In the outer office, as her assistant and the office manager stood between a young man and my agent's office door, he waved something in the air. "I have my SAG card and I've chosen you to be my agent." My first reaction to this statement was to wish I was anywhere but there, as I watched my agent's blood pressure increase so much you could feel it in the air.

Then she wound up and delivered. "Get out of my office! Now!" He looked at her in shock, as she pointed to the door out. He slunk out. I think I started laughing until she gave me a look.

We went back in her office and she regaled me on how ridiculous wannabe actors can be. I guessed correctly that this was not the first time this had happened. She finally laughed and told me that most all of them were extras who got a SAG card by Taft-Hartley vouchers, not by actually acting in anything and believe once they are visited by the SAG Fairy they will instantly be cast in all varieties of film and TV, mostly as the star, and are blessing her by choosing her to represent them. She called it Psycho-SAG-cosis.

This is what a lot of screenwriters think is going to happen when they get an agent or manager.

Nothing could be further from the truth. If you are good enough to get a good manager or agent all they can do is open some doors for you and advise you how to handle those meetings that take place without the manager or agent there. What they do is quite important for sure, but you have to do the rest.

They do not get you jobs.

You get your own jobs by being great in a room, having what the people who you meet with want, and impressing them with your writing talent. If you can do this, then you get to keep your agent or manager who will open more doors for you so you can go out and do it again. Plus, at these meetings your reps set up, it's always good to keep in mind that the person waiting in the outer office when you finish is there to do the same thing. It'll ground you.

Reps also do not sell your scripts.

They can send them to people who can buy them, but they're one of hundreds who are sending their clients' scripts out. Your script quality and being the right script for them at the right time has to sell your script.

Yes, with an agent or manager the "opportunity fairy" can visit a lot more often and that's a very good thing. But you as a writer have to be just as ready for an agent or manager as they are for you. Confident in yourself and your work, not ridiculous big ego confident, but sincerely humble confident. You have to be honest and tell the truth, not just say what you think people want to hear because that always bites you on the butt eventually.

These are the things, besides having some great scripts, that will keep you in good stead with any agent or manager. That and a real work ethic.

Writing one script doesn't make you ready. Being desperate doesn't make you ready. Everything in this business takes time, as I have said dozens of times before. You have to be patient. There is no agent fairy to instantly make you a screenwriting star. Agents and managers are there to work with you in building a career one block at a time. You can't sit back and wait for them to perform miracles, because that's not their job. You're not their only client either. There's nothing magical about it.

So, if you think you're ready, query managers and agents. They are looking for new talent all the time. And keep networking. Referrals work too, if you can get them.

I got my manager through a referral from a director, who was directing one of my films. The manager had to read my work first and talk to me and do all those things they do before agreeing to represent you, but the referral got me through the door. I also got my agent through a recommendation from a producer. A producer who I'd written a successful rewrite for.

Getting an agent or manager is just another steppingstone in managing your own business as a screenwriter. A big one, but one that needs to come at the right time. Knowing that this is a long game, don't be so anxious that you try before you or they are ready.

There are many agent and manager lists online, if you take the time to look, with their emails and information on whether they take unsolicited queries. Some of them don't, and don't say ahead of time, and you'll get emails back telling you this. You move on to the next ones.

You are probably better off looking for a manager first. Managers will often look at new writers who have great scripts. They will often take on new writers. Managers charge 10 to 15% of what you make. They can be producers if they want, so there's always the chance of divided loyalties, and they will often dictate to you what you can and can't write if you want them to send out your scripts. Some of them give you notes and help you develop your scripts. This varies from manager to manager and you need to ask them as many questions as they ask you before signing with them.

I've had managers for years. They have their upsides and downsides. There have been more upsides.

Doesn't mean they're easy to get. You still query producers as you try and find a manager.

Agents are a whole different thing. Agents rarely look at new writers. This is sometimes a hard thing for new writers to swallow, but it's true. Agents look for careers that already exist to make money from. That means you have to have had some success before they'll consider you. Success in selling scripts, getting films made, and those films being critical or financial successes or both. Then they come looking for you.

Agents, by law, take 10% of what you make and can't be producers. They have access to rooms and jobs and producers you do not, and some managers do not. They don't get you jobs, they get you opportunities for those jobs and can send out your scripts. Generally, they don't give you notes or help you develop your work.

How do you query managers and agents?

You still write a very simple query letter.

```
Manager Name,

Thank you for your time. I'm (Your Name
Here). I'm looking for management and
looking at your roster, I feel I'd be a
good fit. I've written a black comedy
thriller       called       Extracurricular
Activities and believe it's a great
sample to send you.

A model high school junior sets all the
curves in all his classes and has an
afterschool job killing parents for his
classmates, frustrating a local cop who
knows, but can't prove it.

It's Ferris Bueller meets Heathers.

Would love to have you read it. Thank
you and let me know if I can send it.

Best,

Your Name here.
```

Again, don't overwrite it. Keep it simple. Stand out from hundreds of overwritten queries these reps get every week from other writers begging for representation.

You may send 100 of these and get three read requests. That's a pretty average return. If they ask you for a read, send the script and…

While you wait, you query producers, because they option and buy scripts on their own if they like them. And make them.

PRODUCERS AND PRODUCTION COMPANIES

I've already talked about how there are tons of producers and production companies out there if you have a low budget script. These are the producers you query.

If you only have your 100-million-dollar budget script, forget it. Go write a couple of low budget ones they'll actually read.

How do you find these producers? There are professional film and screenwriting websites online that you have to pay to access in order to find the information on these producers and companies. Make sure these are legitimate sites by doing your homework. This is the easiest way to find them.

Wait a minute, Bob. Pay money?

Yep. Screenwriting is a business and you are a business owner. Business owners have to invest in their own businesses. You bought screenwriting software, I hope, and that was an investment in your business. These sites are, too. And they are easy to find. Just look.

On one of the sites, you can look up films that are like yours and see who produced those films. You need to find them, then query them with the script that fits best what they do. I have one good friend who got four films made this way.

You send each their personalized query letter and you wait. Again, out of 100 sent, if you get five reads, this is happy territory. These people are getting hundreds of these letters a week.

If you get zero response after a couple of hundred queries, it's time to look at two things.

1. Your logline. Is there any way you can make it better or more interesting?
2. Your premise. Is it really something that would interest a producer? And be honest.

If it's #1, take time to fix it and send more.

If it's #2, move on to your next script to query. You don't beat it into the ground, you move on.

If you get read requests, you send them, and….

Wait.

In three weeks, if you haven't heard, you send a follow up email that looks something like this.

You may, of course, word it your own way, but it needs to be this short.

```
Their Name Here,

Hi, this is Your Name Here, and you
requested my script, Title Here, three
weeks ago. I was wondering if you'd had
a chance to read it yet.

Thank you again for the opportunity,

Your Name Here.
```

And you wait for a reply. If they haven't read it yet, they'll send you an email and tell you this. After that, you never email them again about it.

Why? It's unprofessional and desperate, that's why. If they like it, believe me, they will contact you. If you hear nothing? They've passed.

And you keep sending queries out, even while they're reading it. And writing new scripts.

So now, who else can you send queries to?

Aha, Bob. I know!

ACTORS

Yeah...no. Unless those actors own their own production companies that accept queries, then absolutely you can email them. But actors without production companies? No.

Why, Bob? Maybe they can help me get to producers, if they love it, and can help get it made.

Trying to get actors to attach to your script to make it easier to sell? Yeah, that worked better in the past before there was a Mount Everest of scripts available and all those writers weren't out there trying to get actors, both female and male, to read and promote their scripts.

Their agents get thousands of queries every month. To weed out the real from the wannabes, actor's agents now "field offers", meaning they won't even look at your script unless you have provable funds in the bank to make the film and to pay them to be in your movie. Money. Actual money.

Huh? No, I want the actors to help me get the funds.

Yeah well, that's not happening.

Actors get paid to act by producers, they don't help you find the funds or attach themselves to a film that might never get made. Their job is to get hired by productions with the money to pay them. So they can actually work and pay their bills.

But, but, if they attach themselves, don't they make your script much more attractive to producers? They do, if it's an A-list box office, sure fire star. And there are less than a half a dozen of those. Most actors are just looking for paid work.

Plus, those A-list ones you want have walls surrounding them and agents and managers and assistants on guard 24/7 to keep you away from them.

Unless you have money to pay them. Catch 22, again.

Yes, there are D list actors from TV shows that went off the air ten years ago that are happy to attach to your films, but those actors don't attract producers or money. You might think they would, but you'd be wrong.

Producers help you get the actors you need for your project. Not the other way around, if you're trying to sell your script. If you're making it yourself, you can do whatever you want, but big actors still want to see proof you have the funds to pay them before they'll give you the time of day. It's self-protection.

Ok, actors are mostly out. What about...

DIRECTORS

If they're also producers, sure, you query them. Like any other producer, they do look for scripts. But many of the big-time director/producers also don't accept queries. They get scripts from agents, managers, and referrals from their close friends. You have to do your homework.

If they are not producers? See actors. Just like actors, they get hired by producers who want to choose who they work with, not have you try and choose.

You get to query anyone you want. No one can stop you. But you want your best shot at success. As a new writer, stick with producers and managers. Your read ratio wil be a lot higher.

This is a long frustrating process. You will get discouraged. It's the ones who stay strong and don't give up that have the best shot at prevailing.

CHAPTER 11

HOW NOT TO MARKET YOUR SCRIPT

I think it's time to talk about this subject. I've just told you about query letters and loglines and you're thinking, "There *has* to be a better way. What if I tried...?"

Stop now. There is not a single "What if I tried..." that hasn't been tried. Not one.

And not a single one of them ever worked.

But Bob, I've heard stories about all kinds of crazy things people did that worked and they all became famous writers.

Lies. All lies. Those are all urban legends that have one thing in common. They aren't true and never happened or if they did, were miserable failures opening that writer up to legal problems and/or ridicule.

And always ended with rejection.

So, as a public service to you, I'm going to list ways writers tried to get their scripts out to producers and reps that failed, every time. I do this so you won't think you've thought of something new that has never been done. You haven't.

In no particular order:

The billboard. In the years I've been doing this, this has been tried two or three times. A writer, frustrated that they couldn't sell their script, paid tens of thousands of dollars to have their script, their logline, and their contact info placed on billboards in Hollywood and other places near the studios. It wasn't successful, all I'm gonna say. A very expensive failure. These kinds of things do lead to a lot of very funny social media posts at the expense of the writer and not much else. It's not pretty.

The sandwich board. Standing outside of a studio or an agency headquarters with a sandwich board that has all the details about your script, how great it is, and how they are missing out on something fabulous, is not an optimal way to get your work noticed. Again, a lot of people see it, none of them are thinking they need to read that script. One guy once stood outside a studio gate for a month like this and finally got the message and left when everyone just ignored him the whole time. This has been tried to death. Never worked.

Handing it to a producer, director, or actor in a public place. Like a restaurant, or bar, or sporting event, or on an airplane, or shoving it under a restroom stall door while they are in there, or, you get the picture. If you don't believe the restroom stall door story, a producer told me this happened to him. This is the height of bad taste in any industry. No one has ever sold a script this way, no matter what urban legend you heard. One famous actress once read the riot act to a writer who dropped a script in her lap in public, gathering a crowd, who listened to her tear this writer apart for doing this. You don't want to be that writer.

Taping it to the door of a production company headquarters or talent agency headquarters late at night so they see it in the morning. Done at least once a week somewhere in LA by some clueless writer. They shred it in the morning without reading it or their security people send it back to the writer with a sternly worded legal warning.

The full-page ad in *Variety* or *Billboard.* Expensive and subject to a lot of derisive laughter. One writer even ended their ad with "Let the bidding begin." There was no bidding. And yet, every year someone thinks no one has ever done this, so they try. To more laughter. And the magazines are happy to take your money.

Thinking that handing your script to a relative of a producer or star will get you anywhere. Those relatives know better. They can't accept them and it's embarrassing. Don't even try. This is the worst.

Mailing it to a studio. This includes mailing it to anyone specific in a studio or at a production company or streaming service or producer or, anyone who hasn't requested it. They all keep lists. Trust me. Don't do it. They never get read. Sometimes they get sent back with a nasty legal letter. Sometimes they get shredded without being read. All the time, this doesn't work.

Throwing it over the wall around a producer's or actor's house. Yep. Happens on a pretty regular basis. No one ever sold a script from it. Bird cages do get lined with them.

Having it delivered in an empty pizza box. Sorry, been done to death. One agency tells me they get two to three of these deliveries a week. Plus, your script gets all greasy, but that probably makes them easier to shred.

Handing it to a director or producer or star at a Q&A session for a film, at a film festival, or at a convention. I've seen videos of people trying to do this. Pretty ugly to watch. One director verbally ripped the writer in front of the crowd, who booed the writer out of the room. This happens every time it is tried. It's as embarrassing a thing to do as anything.

Having it delivered with a balloon bouquet or in a flower delivery box. Nope, sorry. A lot of people tried this failed idea before you.

Delivered with a singing telegram. I think it's been done so many times the singing telegram companies have a special screenwriter rate. It's never worked.

Thrown through the open windows of cars driving into the studio gates. A friend of mine at one of the big studios told me about this one. The writer got three through car windows before they arrested him. No one read the script.

Showing up at the studio gate, production company office, or agency headquarters saying you have an appointment. You don't. They know.

Sending gifts with your script. One writer sent a very expensive, probably hundreds of dollars, huge food gift basket to a production company with their script hidden in the bottom of the basket. They threw the script out without looking at it and ate the food. A producer who was there told me this one.

Showing up in a gorilla costume with your script. Or as a knight in armor. Or as the lead character in your script. One guy showed up at a production company in a space suit with his script. Nobody got a script read, much less sold.

Pretending to be your own agent. They're on to this one. They only accept scripts from agencies and agents they know.

Sending the script in an envelope with a big agency's return address and the agency's name on the title page. And they're not your agent. This is a huge no-no. They can tell, too. You go on their list and they tell the agency, who will send you a cease and desist letter and a warning that they will sue you if you do it again, and they put you on their don't read list. These lists exist, put together by each producer, production company, or agency to keep away from people who do things like this.

<u>One guy showed up at an agency as a fireman</u>, telling them he was there to inspect the sprinkler system and fire alarms. Got inside, pulled out his script, got thrown out. Plus, it's against the law to impersonate a firefighter.

<u>Showing up as a UPS or FedEx employee to leave your script.</u> Been done so many times that its why receptionists ask for delivery company ID now. And if you dress as a US mailperson? This one is against federal law, so think twice about that one.

<u>Leaving your script in one of the coffee houses near the studios that producers might frequent</u>, hoping they'll pick it up and read it if it's just sitting there. What really happens? The employees pick it up and read it to each other at lunch and on breaks to laugh at it, then they throw it away.

Here's a couple that defied logic and pretty much assured the writers they'd never have anything read ever…

A writer put his script in a leather briefcase, walked into one of the biggest agencies in the world, and left it in the lobby, thinking someone working there would find it, open it, read the script, and buy it. What really happened? Someone found it and called the LA County Bomb Squad. They emptied floors of the building out. The bomb squad discovered it wasn't a bomb, the Agency sent the bill for the bomb squad to the writer. The script never got read. The writer got put on the "don't read" list.

And finally, two writers wrote a comedy script they couldn't get anyone to read, so they sent it out with a famous writer's name on the cover sheet as the writer instead of them, and then, I think on the last page, revealed, *Aha*, this isn't the famous writer's script *at all*, but *ours*! *Surprise!!!* It made all the industry media and was not received well by the industry or the writer they tried to impersonate. It was pretty much a disaster. The script didn't sell.

I'm sure there are more, but you get the idea. These all have been done and all have failed.

I'll let you in on a secret. Corporately, the agencies and production companies and producers have a policy to never read any scripts they get any other way but the ways they've expressed approval of. None. Why? Because if they did, it would open flood gates of craziness they don't want to deal with and won't deal with.

Don't do these things.

I cannot stress enough how bad this looks to the people you hope to impress.

You also need to know this….

<u>Things not to do if you get a read request from a producer or rep:</u>

Never send anything but the script.

Or if it's a pilot and they want your mini-Bible? Send that too. Nothing else.

Here's a list anyway, in case you think you're the exception. Clue: you aren't, and these have been sent in with scripts in the past to disastrous results.

Never send with your script:

1. A list of your music choices for the film or a CD of the music with marks in the script when to start the next song as you read.
2. A list of your casting choices for the characters, including pictures.
3. Your ideas of how you'd film it as the director, including a book of pictures.
4. Maps of the fantasy world or a book with the history of the fantasy world you created in the script.
5. Charts or graphs of anything.
6. Cute or funny props that are in the script.
7. Food or wine. Hint: they won't read the script, but they'll drink the wine.
8. Hats or shirts with the script name on them.

My philosophy on marketing your script? As long as it's not illegal, immoral, or stupid, go for it. All of the above fall well into the stupid category and some in the illegal category.

People who can read your scripts are pretty smart and they've been around this business long enough to have seen it all. There is nothing they haven't seen and nothing you could think of outside the way they want scripts delivered to them that will work. Clever delivery methods have never resulted in an exception to their company policies. No company with a "no unsolicited submissions" policy gets an unsolicited submission delivered creatively and goes, "Wow. You fooled me. I've never seen that tried before. I have to read this." Whether a script comes by UPS or unicycle, a company will send the same "we don't accept unsolicited submissions" response either way. Glad that's out of your system.

WRITING SCRIPTS YOU DON'T OWN THE RIGHTS TO

While I'm talking about things you shouldn't do, let me get this out of the way, too.

Yes, for your own enjoyment, you can write anything you want. If you want to write a superhero film based on your favorite comic book or movie characters? Or your favorite space adventure? Or a sequel to your favorite movie or TV show? Or anything that's already been done that's not in public domain?

You absolutely can do this and get it out of your system. The problem comes when you decide you want to make them or sell them or get them to the companies that own those rights. That you cannot do. They will not read them, they will not buy them, and most likely you'll get what's called a "cease and desist" letter from their attorneys.

If you persist, they will sue you. They have done this. It's called Copyright Infringement and in some cases is also Trademark Infringement. You cannot win these suits.

One of the larger studios has an entire four story building full of lawyers just looking for people who infringe on their copyrights and trademarks so they can sue them if they don't stop.

Write something original and this will never happen.

Remember:

You need to believe in the power of your scripts. Your words. Your stories. Trust that if you write something genuinely great someone will recognize it for what it is. You need to get it out there the way producers and reps want it done. That's what works. All this other stuff doesn't.

You won't be the exception, so be businesslike. It's the way the industry work.

CHAPTER 12

MARKETING YOUR SCRIPT, part two

Besides the query, which you should be doing no matter what else you try, there are a few other ways to get your script read.

<u>NETWORKING</u>

Let's get something out of the way first: what networking is *not*.

Networking is *not* meeting someone in the industry and instantly asking or expecting them to help you succeed. That's using people. And surprise!!! No one has the deep secret desire to be used that way. No one.

Networking is *not* going to an industry event or party or screening with a script under your arm to give out. Or with business cards to give out, unless someone specifically asks. Industry people are there, away from work, to enjoy themselves. Having to run from people who want something is not enjoyable.

Networking is *not* going on some screenwriting board or Twitter and after having a known writer answer your question or comment on something you said, then using his/her name to as a personal reference to try to get your script read. This has happened way more than once and again, surprise, producers, agents, and managers check references.

This has happened to me twice, with producers calling me asking if I knew writers who had used my name as a reference to get them to read their scripts. Both times I had no idea who these people were. The producer got mad. I got mad. The scripts were ignored and he gave me the emails of both writers so I could tell them how unhappy I was. I did tell them. I never heard back from either of them.

Networking is *not* expecting anybody to do anything for you, especially people you don't know.

So, what is networking?

It's all about building relationships. Period. Afterward, it's about your skill as a writer, delivering something worth the help you can get eventually from those friends. You can network fabulously, but if your scripts are lacking, it won't matter. Make sure your scripts are ready before you use the network you've built.

We've all, in our lives, built relationships with people. Emphasis on *built*. People who became lifelong friends. Or friends who for any number of reasons end up being temporary relationships. Or friends you make and lose touch with, but still have meaning to you. You can quantify every one of those friends. You care about them. If it's a true relationship, they care about you, too.

Business relationships work the same way. You know the person you're dealing with and trust them because that trust has been built. It's not instant. It's a bond that takes time and effort and sincerity.

And that's where I lose a lot of screenwriters.

Time? I don't have time. I want my script sold now. My mom loves it and thinks it should get made. Have you seen the stuff that gets made? My time is now.

Effort? Hey! I just spent a good part of maybe a month writing this script. You have no idea how much effort that was. Effort to get someone to help me? No way. They should want to help me because they're already there and I'm not.

Sincerity? If they can't help me now, I don't care about them. They owe every writer help to get ahead, especially me. They're successful, they can help me. Me. It's about me.

I've been to industry gatherings and parties and screenings. I've seen the best and worst of networking. I'm not surprised that the best networkers and most sincere people are usually the best writers. They've made the effort to understand what it takes to be successful beyond having written great scripts. They're at these gatherings to foster good relationships within the industry. To meet people. To get to know people as people, not as faceless beings who can help them. And if that sincere networking ends with them getting some mutual business benefit from it at some later point, great. If not, great too, because you've still got maybe a real friend out of it.

When you network correctly, you have to throw your ambition out the door for a while. Not in a calculated way either. Really toss it. Network to learn. Network to grow. Network to build your circle of friends.

Again. You need to get to know people as people. I know this sounds ridiculous on the face of it because you're thinking, "Well, duh." But a lot of writers forget that successful writers and producers and agents and managers and some actors are just people, with lives and interests outside the industry. Nobody wants to talk business all the time. Nobody. And nobody in the industry is dying to help you. They just aren't.

Successful industry people all have their radar permanently on, watching for people who would try and use them. They have to. It happens more than you could ever imagine. Like, every day, multiple times a day, more. The second they even get a whiff of it, you can see it in their eyes as they glaze over with the thought, "Not again." I've seen it. Heck, I've experienced it from both sides. Don't think I didn't make some horrendous networking mistakes in my young career when in my stupid ego induced state. I thought some people were living their lives just to help me. It wasn't until someone who loved my writing pulled me aside and set me straight about making a jerk out of myself. And luckily, I listened instead of letting my ego rule and ruin everything.

And my eyes have glazed over when I've been confronted by writers who wanted my list of contacts or for me to pass a script to producers or to my manager the very first time I met them. And no, I didn't do any of it. What I did do was get away from them as fast as I could.

You get to know people. You have genuine interest in who they are. You treat them with the respect they deserve. The same respect you want back.

Don't go to industry parties or industry gatherings with a thumb drives full of scripts. If you offer your business card to people, they will take it, so they don't have to talk to you any further. Honest. Those cards go into the closest trash can after you walk away. I had a producer tell me once that getting a business card was sometimes the quickest way out of a conversation they didn't want to be in, because the person they were talking to saw them as a pathway to what they wanted and not as a person.

Networking is an art. It's about being real. It's about listening more than talking. It's about asking questions that show you're interested in the person you're talking to beyond what you think you can get out of them.

Networking is a slow dance. A lot of times with someone who doesn't want to dance with you at first. They've seen it all and they don't like what they've seen. So, you don't walk up and grab their arm and pull them onto the dance floor to dance to *your* song. That never works and can hurt you in ways that can kill a career. You sincerely get to know them over time so that when their song comes on, they don't mind when you ask them to dance.

Oh, and you still have to have a great script at the end of the dance.

SOCIAL MEDIA

Social media, for me, has been a very good place to network. I've met two fabulous writing partners there, one of whom I wrote a script with that got sold and made. I've met a host of amazing writers I'm now very close friends with, some wonderful producers and showrunners who are friends. And they're friends I may never work with.

There's a thing called Screenwriting Twitter. It's not really anything but a bunch of screenwriters who follow each other on Twitter.

You find screenwriters you like on there and follow them. And when they post stuff you like, you "like" what they said. Look who responds to them. Who they answer and talk to. Follow those people. On rare occasions, comment on their threads. But don't be false and don't overdo it. Over time, they'll see you're not after anything and they'll start to respond to you. This is when you start making friends. Real friends.

I've met a bunch of lovely people and outstanding writers there who I'm happy to cheer on in their careers, who I have gone on to know away from social media in real life. It's genuine friendships. I want them to succeed.

It took me years to get to know them and them to know me. It was a slow process of building trust. Networking is not a shortcut.

There are other screenwriting boards all over the Internet. There are some great people on them. There are people you wouldn't want to know, ever. There are people looking to take advantage of you. You have to take your time and see who is who and weed out the good from the bad. You have to be careful. If something looks too good to be true, it always is.

You'll also see and hear a lot of stuff about screenwriting you'll know is dead wrong. You'll hear great advice from writers who are experienced. You'll get false sage advice from people who have never optioned or sold a script, but act like they know everything. You'll see the bitter, the desperate, the happy, and everyone in between.

You have to be careful and listen. You'll find people there that want to do what you want to do. Kindred spirits. You'll find people who can eventually help you. You'll find people who will want you to help them. It's networking at its best and worst. It's the Internet, so you have to take it all with a healthy set of skepticism.

You can find some amazing friends and colleagues there. I have.

FILM FESTIVALS

Every time a bell rings, a new film festival comes into being.

Not quite, but close. Every area of the country has them now. They're great places to network and meet new people with the same interests as you. Yes, you may have to pay to get into them or to attend the afterparties. But there will be people there who you can meet and network with. You never know who you will meet there. This is if you just want to attend. If you have a film in competition the networking can even be better.

One more thing. Don't take any of your scripts to any of the events. That scares people away.

As you look into these festivals, do your homework and try to get to the screenwriter-centric ones. They do exist. Enter your scripts into their competitions. They all have them. Producers won't care if you do well in them, but at the festivals themselves you will meet people as a winner you might never meet otherwise.

This also means you need to get yourself to the ones you win. So, if your funds are tight, make the ones you enter closer to where you live. They don't pay your way or for your hotel. It doesn't do you any good to win the *Maine Film Festival* script competition if you live in Nevada and can't get to Maine. Being there is the only thing that counts at these kinds of festivals when it comes to networking.

Film festivals are great places to network, to meet people, to start long term relationships.

PITCH FESTS

I'm not a fan. I don't like anything where you have to pay to get your work seen. Well, in this case, your two-minute pitch heard. Being good at your pitch is a wonderful thing, but paying to do it? It strikes me as a moneymaker for everyone but the writer, in my opinion.

You can choose to do these, but it's a buyer beware situation. I've spoken to a lot of writers who did this once and that was enough. No one I personally know or have talked to about them has ever gotten any traction out of one of these. Do your homework. Look online for stories of people who have attended and read what they have to say. And if you still want to do it? I hope it works for you.

SCREENWRITING CONTESTS

There are hundreds of them. You can spend a fortune entering them all. There are a couple I can personally recommend because I know for a fact that producers pay attention to those. I cannot speak to any others because I don't know, and it's better to say "I don't know" than to speak from ignorance.

I've only heard the producers and reps I know speak of two they pay attention to. *The Nicholl*, run by the Motion Picture Academy. Yes, the Oscar people. If you make it to even the semi-finals of this contest, you can get some reads from producers and reps. The finals or win it? Just about everyone in LA that counts will read your script.

Close to 8,000 scripts are entered into *The Nicholl* each year. Because of the sheer numbers, you have to have a script that's way above average to do well. I have had personal friends who made the Finals, and a couple of them got their scripts sold and made. It's also one of the few contests where your script is read twice by two different judges at each level.

Go online and look at the rules and when the contest starts. If you have a great script, it's the one you shoot for. It's also only for amateurs, as professional writers are excluded. So, you have an even playing field.

The other contest I've personally heard producers like is the *Austin Film Festival Screenwriting Contest*. Austin is a completely screenwriter-centric festival. It's all about screenwriting and winning that competition can get you a lot of reads.

There are zero guarantees of success from any contest, but the opportunity is there. You have to make sure your script is mega ready though, because every year the numbers of scripts submitted goes up.

Now a word of warning. Do not tout your script as an "award winner" unless you actually win a contest. They check if you claim this. Quarterfinals and semi-finals do not make your script an award winner in the eyes of producers or reps. It does make them roll their eyes, however, if you claim your script as award winning with just these finishes.

PAID SCRIPT POSTING SITES

There are a couple of sites online where you can pay to post your scripts and one of them does reviews and rates the scripts. Yes, a very small percentage of scripts put on these sites get optioned or writers get reps from it. It has happened and will happen again. *A very small percentage.*

It's no different than the odds on getting optioned or repped from a query letter. Very small. But it does happen. Query letters are cheaper. You do have some steep out of pocket investments if you want to go the pay posting route. It's your choice.

In the spirit of transparency, I used one of these services a few years ago and optioned a script to a large production company. They never made the film and I got it back, but it did work for me.

One of them is really for micro and small budget films, as those are mostly the kinds that have had success there. Again, if you want to spend the money, about the same results as from queries.

RECOMMENDATIONS

I got my manager and my agent through recommendations from a director and a producer. It was years and years into my career, because it's very hard to get reps and it was through these recommendations that these particular reps met with me, looked at my work, my past successes, and eventually took me on as a client.

How did I manage to get these recommendations? The director loved one of my scripts and optioned it and because we became real friends, he recommended me to a manager. Networking.

The producer was someone I did a hired rewrite for on the recommendation of another producer. He loved my work and we worked well together. He recommended me to an agent. Networking.

In both cases, I asked them if they could recommend me to someone they knew after we had established our own relationships. Both were happy to.

The lesson here is that no one knows what you want or need until you tell them. It's all about timing and the nature of your relationships. It's not a bad thing to ask someone for something like this after working together successfully. The mistake new writers make is asking for these kinds of things right off the bat. That doesn't work.

So, these things take time and work and happen after you've established yourself in some way. Something you'll have to do without reps.

SELLING IDEAS

Let's get his one out of the way, too.

I cannot tell you the number of times I've heard, "I have these movie ideas that are better than anything out there. How do I get them to a studio so I can collect my millions?"

Movie ideas. When I was working on the set of *Nash Bridges* for those six seasons, everybody had an idea or script: the guy who watered the plants, the dolly grip, the extras, the boom operator, the set decorator. I read his script, it wasn't bad. You name it, they had a script or an idea to sell.

Now, to be truthful again, I also had ideas and scripts then, too. I was also trying to get them to anyone who would pay attention, like everyone else. So, I'm not denigrating the people who want to see their films or ideas made, ok? That I understand.

There's a difference between an idea and the culmination of that idea in a finished script. Ideas have no value until they become scripts, if you're a new writer.

There are always those out there who just want to sell the ideas.

I guess what I don't understand is the non-willingness to work for it. I once heard someone say, "I have the best ideas for films Hollywood's ever seen, but I just want to sell the ideas, because writing a script would be too much work."

I was happy to tell this person how they could do that. "First", I told him, "you have to move to Fantasyland."

What he was looking for was a shortcut to success. He'd think of an idea, one or two sentences of a premise, then the studios, who have bags of money just lying around, would dip into those bags and give him untold dollars and send him on his way while they hired a writer to write his fabulous idea and a director to direct it and then he'd go to the premiere and see his name on the screen.

See what I mean about Fantasyland?

Everybody everywhere has a movie idea. I run into people with movie ideas all the time when they find out what I do for a living. I tell them what I will tell you: Nobody buys ideas. They buy the execution of those ideas. They buy your hard work turning that idea into a wham bang script.

But Bob, I read in the trade papers about a writer who sold a pitch.

Yes, writers sell pitches. But the producers who buy those pitches are buying the writer who pitched it as much as the idea. They know that particular writer can take that idea and make it something special because they have an extensive track record of doing just that. I've sold a pitch. I've sold a few. But I sold them to production companies I had already sold finished scripts to and had done multiple writing assignments for. They knew what I could do with the idea. I earned that right with years and years of hard work.

If you want to sell an idea, write the script. That's the only way to sell your idea as a new or not established writer.

WRITING A NOVEL TO HELP SELL YOUR SCRIPT

Taking your script and writing a novel from it has popped up as a way some writers think they can get noticed faster. "The script is based on my novel." Like this will generate more interest in your script.

So, as a public service, I'll tell you how producers react to this, based on my experience and what I've heard directly from them and production company execs.

Their first question is not ever about the book's content. The first question they ask is, "How many have you sold?" That's right. And you'd better have a quick honest answer. In this case, "I don't know" isn't acceptable.

If it's under 50,000, they don't really care if you have a novel or not. For the novel to be important to them, they want that built-in audience the book has generated to sell tickets or streaming views, nothing more.

If your book has sold that many copies, first of all, good for you. Secondly, you might get some interest in the book. Producers option novels all the time, then hire writers they know to adapt the book to script form.

I personally know two authors who had screenplays based on their novels already written when their novels were optioned and neither time did the producers even want to read their scripts. They wanted to hire their own writers to adapt the book.

This business doesn't ever take into consideration your expectations. Like I said before, when they option or buy something, it's theirs to do with as they please.

So, if you're counting on the fact that there's a novel your script is based on to make a difference in your screenwriting career? Better start marketing the heck out of your book and sell a lot of copies. From there, it's a crap shoot whether they'll even want to see your script based on the book.

Wish this was different, but it's not.

SENDING YOUR REQUESTED SCRIPT

Now, you've done all of this and someone has let you know they want to read your script. How do you handle that? Simple. You send a PDF of your script attached to an email that says,

```
Producer or Rep name here,

Attached is the screenplay "Your Script
Title" as you requested. Thank you for
taking the time to read it.

Your name.
```

That's it. They don't want to read how excited you are or how much a fan of theirs you are, or how happy your mom or kids are about this, or how it will win a Golden Globe, or do a billion at the box office. Keep it short. Sweet. Professional.

You'll also be tempted to write something in the email explaining the script or story more. Don't do this. They'll think "If they need to explain it to me again after I've already requested it, how good can it be?" You don't want them to read it with that mindset.

Let your script be the center of all attention, not you.

Then you:

SUBMIT AND FORGET

After a couple of years of making the mistake of sitting by the phone or computer and worrying daily about every submitted script, I finally made the choice to submit and forget. It changed my life.

No more worrying about whether a producer likes or doesn't like my script. I know if they do, I'll be hearing from them.

For my own self-preservation, I adopted this mindset. It works.

So, if you get a read request, Submit and Forget. And keep trying to get that same script out. And write a new one. Or rewrite your old ones. Don't wait around for answers. You owe no one an exclusive. You owe yourself the freedom not to drive yourself crazy waiting. Beyond that one email reminder three weeks in, it's not healthy to do anything but let it go.

I should have done this long before I did. When I was acting and auditioning a lot, I used to fret about every audition and wait and wait by the phone for the answer. And one day, before an audition I couldn't believe I got, for a film I really wanted to be in, for a director I really wanted to work for, I realized the chances of me actually getting the part were probably as close to zero as you can get. It was a liberating moment, I thought, "If I'm not going to get it, I'm going to just go in there and have fun." And I did. And I got the part.

Revelation.

So, the next 8 auditions I went on, I did the same thing, same mindset. I'm not going to get it so relax and have fun. I auditioned nine times over that period and got all nine parts. My agent said at the time it was a record for her. When I audition now, even though it's a rare thing, I still have the same mindset. I get most of what I audition for.

Took me longer to realize the same mindset could help relieve the stress of submitting a script. Chances are overwhelming the answer is going to be a No, so now I send it and forget it. Much healthier.

The people you submit your scripts to are happily living their lives and aren't worried about what you're putting yourself through at all. They not only don't think about it, they actively don't care and never will. The only one putting stress on you is you. Don't do it. Don't spend valuable time you can't get back worrying about something you have zero control over.

Submit it and Forget it.

BREAKING IN

I get asked all the time how I broke in. What did I do to market myself and my scripts?

I used networking to get my writing seen. It took years, even with the contacts I made through my acting career. I endured rejection after rejection. I had to be endlessly patient and never lose sight of my goal.

A produced film with my name on it as the writer. Your goal, too.

I did any kind of writing I could. I wrote commercials for the radio station I worked for. Yes, I did a short weird three-year stint as an on-air disk jockey.

I wrote industrial films. Those are the films corporations make for internal use or for their customers. I wrote instructional videos. I wrote infomercials. I wrote anything that people would pay me to write.

I took low paying rewrite jobs on independent films from India that were filming in the US. I took low paying rewrite jobs on some independent films that never got made and on some films that got made and never got distribution. Films nobody saw.

I wrote and wrote more spec scripts and marketed myself relentlessly, but not stupidly. I networked the right way and eventually I wrote a script a whole bunch of people wanted. It opened doors. But it took years and years for those open doors to pay off in any meaningful way.

I talk to my friends who are successful writers and they tell the same story with a slightly different route each one traveled. The main thing that's the same for all of us? The excruciatingly long time it took.

Screenwriters see success, on average, with their ninth script. And, it takes an average of about 8 years from the time you write a script to the time it gets made. I'm not making these numbers up. It's the industry. It moves at a snail's pace. Putting a film together takes a miracle.

Take it from me though, miracles do happen. They're just not instant.

Extracurricular Activities took 18 years from the time I wrote it to the time the film got made. *The Right Girl* took four years. The others somewhere in between.

A friend was a finalist in the *Nicholl* and it took his winning script 8 years to get made.

Other friends with hot scripts and pilots according to the Hollywood trade papers are still in the development process on those projects five to 10 years in.

I tell you these hard facts because I don't want you to think you're going to be the exception and get there quickly just because you want to.

YOU'RE NOT GOING TO BE THE EXCEPTION

But you don't understand, Bob. I am going to be the exception. I know it in my heart. I'm breaking in fast. It's going to work for me because I'm brilliant and my script is brilliant and my film needs to be seen by audiences everywhere, right now. My mom says so, too.

I can't tell you how many times I've read or heard or seen exactly this attitude. Then when their script gets no traction, it's always everything but the script's fault.

I will say what I always say and will continue to say, "Great scripts find a way." They don't always get made, but they can make careers. It's never fast and you wanting it to be faster isn't going to make it so. There will be bumps and bruises galore along the way. You'll be frustrated.

You aren't going to be the exception because there are, statistically speaking, none. You hear a story about some new writer who sold their script for big money? Chances are that writer spent years networking and querying to get it read and it was one of those fabulous rare amazing scripts that comes along once every few years, and then the writer was great in the room. The perfect storm. Nothing you can count on or anticipate for yourself. And it was probably that writer's 8th script.

Most writers who you hear are "Overnight Successes," and I personally know a couple of them, laugh at that thought, knowing how hard and for how many years they worked to get there.

Stop thinking you'll be the exception. It will slow your progress. Trust it'll be a long process, then when it happens you can be excited and not disappointed it took so long. It's all about not giving up.

Remember:

All these marketing avenues are rinse and repeat territory. You never stop. You keep networking. You enter more than one script into the contests that count. You improve on the script that made the quarterfinals last year and enter it again the next year. You keep going to meet-ups and film festivals.

Marketing your work is never ending, even after you're successful. Plus, you have to keep writing new scripts. That's a screenwriter's life.

CHAPTER 13

WHAT WILL I GET PAID? SALES & OPTIONS

I have no idea exactly how much you'll get paid. But I have a pretty good idea and it won't be a million dollars. So, get that out of your head right now.

You probably won't be getting WGA wages or residuals either, unless you sell to a guild affiliated producer or production company using a guild contract. The WGA, or Writers Guild is a union of screenwriters. You have to qualify to join via a points system that you can look up on their web site. It's not easy, but if your career advances the way you want it to, you'll probably end up a member someday.

No, if you register your script with the WGA that doesn't mean you're a member. I've heard this fallacy enough that I have to include this here.

One thing you need to know about the union because I think it's important.

You don't want to become a member of the WGA before you're ready. Unlike service unions, they don't help get you jobs. There's no union hall where they choose the next writer in line for the jobs available. You have to get those jobs yourself. They don't find you an agent or manager. You have to get those for yourself. And any of those cool small jobs you got on independent films? Those are gone now. You can't work on non-union jobs. You are restricted to union jobs only. Which is the way it should be as a union member.

As a member, that means you're now competing with the best writers in the world for those union only jobs. To be clear, those jobs aren't open to everyone in the WGA. A select few writers get to go in and compete for each one, the list chosen by the employer, not the WGA. There are a whole lot of writers who got in the WGA before they were ready and never worked again. Being in the WGA does not guarantee you will work a day or, actually, any day. That's on you.

So, how do you approach it?

Working your way to it over time, gaining experience working on non-union projects, gaining the respect of producers, gaining a reputation for good work. That's what you want to do. Then you're ready to compete and ready for the WGA.

So, what does the WGA do then? The WGA guarantees wages, which is a very good thing, and has a good medical plan if you reach their yearly earning goals, and a retirement plan that you need to qualify for. They collectively negotiate wages and writing conditions with producers for the writers in their guild. They negotiate residuals and decide on screen credits.

That's a very basic look at them. They're a good organization that helps and supports their members. It's a logical step for writers who are ready to join and qualify.

WGA pay is on a scale you can easily look up, but the chances of your first sale or job being WGA are really pretty slim. It happens, but only in very select circumstances, like you have a brilliant amazing script that will attract a Guild signatory producer or production company, and those scripts are rare. It does happen, but it's nothing you should count on.

Back to pay.

So, for this exercise, I'll talk about non-union films. Which are most non-studio independent films. Which are most films, period.

Ok. Ok. We get it, but Bob, what will I get paid?

Let's get this out of the way first: Writers don't set their prices for their scripts. You don't put a price tag on your screenplay and set it on a table somewhere. That's not the way it works. Writers get offers from producers and production companies. Then you negotiate from there. You can walk away if you don't get what you want. So can producers if they don't want to pay what you're asking. Producers do walk away, by the way, just so you know.

Have I walked away from deals over money? Yes. Was I sorry afterward? No. But it was later in my career. When I was first starting, would I have walked from that same deal? Nope. Not on your life.

The truth is, new non-union screenwriters get paid very little for their first scripts or writing jobs. The average writer pay on a low budget film, a 1 to $5 million production, can be as low as $5 to $10,000 for a first script. You might get offered more. It's always negotiable.

On a micro budget $50 to $250,000 film? Anywhere from $100 to $500, maybe up to $3000 on a $500,000 film,

You aren't getting rich. You're building a career.

So, the next question is, why is the pay so low? Because the writer is an unknown quantity. They buy the writer as much as they buy a script. Why do you think they want to meet with writers before they option or buy a script? To see if they want to work with you. If yes, then they make an offer.

What you can do for them, as a new writer in production mode, is a question only answered after the script is optioned or sold and development begins. Can you handle rewrites, especially radical rewrites, the way directors and producers want? Most new writers cannot. Just a fact.

So, the pay is low because in the budget they have to include pay for the writers they have to bring in to rewrite your script after they let you go. They have to make room for that. They do it by paying less for a script by an unknown writer with unknown production writing ability.

Do the writers brought in to rewrite the script get paid more than the original writer did? Yes, about 98% of the time they do. Sometimes three to four times as much, sometimes more, sometimes a lot more. Why? Because their worth has been proven to producers and directors time and again. They worked their way up to that kind of status and money. Don't think for a second they didn't start at the bottom at one point. I did. Every writer has.

What? What other writers? Let me go? From my own script? What does that mean?

New writers have to prove their worth. It's not just about the script. It's about the writer's ability to work under pressure and to take notes, implement those notes, and to be open and cooperative. To act like a professional. Most new writers are sadly lacking in these things to start. Some learn them over time and thrive. Some don't.

If you can't do these things. They thank you very much for writing the original script and tell you they don't need your services on the project anymore. This has happened to every writer you've ever heard of. It's a standard practice in this business. It's done daily.

And nothing for you to worry about until you option or sell a script.

OPTIONS

Outright script sales are extremely rare these days. Producers will option your script first if they are interested in it.

What's an option? My best definition is that it's a "rent to own" program. You get a contract that says they will exclusively rent your script for 6, 12, or 18 months to see if they can get financing, actors, or directors attached to it, and get it greenlit. They usually have a renewal or extension built in for the same amount of time, an extension they can take if they're making progress on it.

And by exclusively, I mean you cannot shop that script or show it to any other producers during this time frame. It no longer belongs to you. They are actually renting the complete rights to it for that time period.

I can read your mind right now, you're saying, wait a second, they get to rent my script exclusively for up to three years to see if they'll even make it?

No, sometimes they build in two renewals and they can have it up to 4 ½ years. For this rental, a lot of producers will ask you to do it for, *free*. If they can get away with it.

Or a dollar. I'm not a fan of these kinds of options. I think writers, even new writers, can ask for more. Should ask for more. Even if it's $100 to $500 to start and the same for each renewal, or more if you can get it. It makes the producers own some skin in the game. A real, even if small, investment in your script. It's easier to write off something you got for free.

Then, if they make a film based on your script during this option time, there's a sale price built into the option agreement they will pay you. An amount for the sale you've agreed to. Back to those sale numbers above. You negotiate the sale price into the option agreement. When they decide to make the film during this period, it's called "exercising the option." They can do this at any time during the option period and you have to take the sale price you agreed to.

Ok, but what if they don't make the film by the time the option runs out?

You get the original script back to option or sell again.

Wait? What? They can rent my script for up to 4 ½ years and just hand it back after paying me, nothing? Like it never happened?

Yep. Or you can make $300 to $1500, then get it back.

And something did happen. Someone liked your work enough to try and get it made. It just didn't work. I've optioned a lot of scripts that didn't get made. Every successful writer has. It's part of the business. You never really get used to it. Each one hurts, but you learn to get over it.

Here's some other bad news, a huge percentage of optioned scripts never get made. Quite a few sold scripts don't get made either. As of this writing I have three film scripts and one TV pilot I've sold that I'm pretty sure will never get made. It happens and as the writer you have zero control over it.

If you're looking at screenwriting as a way to wealth, stop now. Can you make a great living from it? Yes, you can. Over time. Mostly, a long time. Can you get wealthy? A very select few writers get wealthy and only after many many years working in the industry successfully.

All of it takes time and proving yourself, over and over. You have to start on the ground floor. Again, you are not getting a million dollars for your first script. You may sell a dozen of them and never make close to that much for any one of them.

So, lower your money sights when you're first starting. It will help you when reality strikes and help you to not make mistakes in dealing with producers the first time. A lot of deals have died because first time writers had unrealistic expectations.

That said, never give your scripts away or option your scripts for free. You do deserve to get paid, even if it's a hundred dollars. And don't be fooled by "back end" deals.

You will get producers who offer you "net points" instead of pay. Net points, in my opinion, are a lovely trap for new writers because they rarely ever pay off. In my world of writers, I've never met a single one who got net points money. Get your money up front. If they want to pay you net points after you get what you want in up front pay, that's fine. Never in place of.

You will also get offers of "deferred pay". This means you're writing for free. Trust me. I have never met anyone who got paid on a "deferred pay" deal. Get something up front.

You will get offers of "IMDb credit and Exposure". Both of these things are basically worthless and the producers offering it know this. They count on your desperation. Don't fall for it. It's better to not sell a script than give it away, in my opinion.

They plan on making money from your script, why shouldn't you?

SHORTS

I get asked if all these things apply to short film scripts. No. They don't. Getting paid for them rarely happens. Sometimes you can make $50-$100 for a short film script. But here's the rub....

Short films are mostly director calling cards. They're resumes from directors saying, "Look what I can do," and they rarely help writers. Producers don't really look at who wrote short films, just at who directed them. I wish this wasn't true, but it is.

If you're a writer/director, that's a different thing and short films can help you if you win festivals with them. You can get noticed.

YOUR RIGHTS

I have rights as a screenwriter?

I know that's what you're asking on seeing this heading.

Yes. You do.

It's your signature on any contract you get. No one makes you sign it. And real producers, not the fakey ones who just want to fleece you and they exist, are happy to deal with you on an equal basis. If a producer calls you and wants to meet with you, that means they think you belong in the room with them.

That means you get to ask them as many questions as they ask you. You can ask what they've produced before. You can ask what kind of budget they see for your film. You can ask who they see playing the roles.

You can ask, Anything within reason.

What's *not* within reason to ask and is perceived as unprofessional and naive?

1. Asking to direct the film if you've never directed anything. If you have, you can have this discussion.
2. Asking to act in the film, especially to star in it. This has killed a lot of projects before they got anywhere. Rocky was 40+ years ago and times have changed.
3. Asking to contractually be the only writer on the project. They never agree to this and will walk away if you insist on it.
4. Asking for script approval, that you have to approve any script changes. They will laugh you out of the room, and you'd really be out of the room, forever.
5. Casting approval or to have anything to do with casting your film (instant no).
6. That you can be on set for the shoot. (that's a discussion for later.)

I know what you're thinking,

What? I can't pick the actors? Or be in it? Or have script approval?

Painful lesson #1: No. Writers, even top writers, don't get to do these things. And don't bring up the exceptions, you'll never be the exception. Honest. J.K. Rowling sold a billion copies of her books, you sell a billion copies of your books, you can have script approval too.

Hold on a second, Bob, you've acted in some of your films.

Yes, but I didn't ask. They asked me. They also knew I'd been in front of a few cameras before. When you establish relationships, these things can happen. New writers can't assume they will or ask for them. Optioning or selling a script will have to be enough to start.

What about directing?

Painful lesson #2: Unless you have a slew of examples of your directing ability with either successful festival short films you've directed, or a low budget film you directed, (oh, it has to be good, too) and/or some film school experience? They won't even talk to you about it. Why? Because finance people don't invest in untested, inexperienced directors and good actors don't put themselves in the hands of untested, inexperienced directors. I've seen projects die early deaths from this. I've talked to actors who turned down good roles because it was a first-time director.

So, what can you ask for besides money? It doesn't mean you'll get it, but you can ask for it. And this only goes for non-union contracts.

1. Guaranteed writing credit. This they can give you if you ask for it. It's been in every one of my non-union contracts.
2. That's about it.

CONTRACTS

I am not a lawyer. I am not going to give anyone legal advice. I have contract experts who read my contracts and give me guidance.

But I can tell you:

Never sign a contract under pressure. Real producers give you time to read it, get it to lawyers to read, or get it to reps to read. No legitimate producer asks you to sign a contract quickly. When a producer does this, you think twice about doing business with them and double check everything, taking as much time as you need.

I once had contract negotiations for the sale of a TV pilot take over two months. It's give and take, and understanding that you as the writer are in an equal position in negotiations. You get to ask about contract items. You get to ask them to change things. They get to say, "Ok" or "No" or "How about this?" and you get to decide whether you can live with it. Will you have to agree to money and parts of your first contract you wish were better? You will. I still sign contracts I'm not 100% happy with, but that are still acceptable. I understand the other side of the equation. The producer's side of it. It's a business. Never forget that.

So, as a businessperson, you always read the whole contract, word for word, yourself. Some of mine have been 30+ pages. Didn't matter. I read them. Every word.

As you read, you highlight the stuff you don't understand or don't like or both. You pay money, if you have to, to have a qualified entertainment attorney look at your contracts. If you have a friend or family member that's a lawyer, great. If not, hire one. Once you sign a contract, you can't take it back. And don't fall for using the producer's free lawyer to look at it for you. Being cheap can cost you a lot.

It's your name on the contract, so be knowledgeable and comfortable with what you're signing and don't sign the first thing put in front of you. That's like paying sticker price for a car. You don't do that, no matter how excited you are about that new car smell.

Can you make a living as a writer? Yes. I do. Took me more than a decade of trying, but yes. Your mileage may vary. It's a long hard slog, but worth it when you get there.

CHAPTER 14

REJECTION

Reject: *a*: to refuse to accept, consider, submit to, take for some purpose, or use *<rejected the suggestion>* *<reject a manuscript>*

The official *Miriam Webster* definition of the word "reject" actually includes "reject a manuscript". It's part of the official definition of the word.

Isn't that instructive?

I actually laughed when I read it, looking it up for this book. But when you think about it, it makes all the sense in the world. Rejection is the one constant in any screenwriter's life. It's with us daily. Whether we're dreading it or mourning it or anticipating it, it lives with us, taunting us.

Am I making it seem like more than it is? I don't think so. Most non-writers wouldn't understand how personal it feels when someone says, "We're going to pass on your incredibly hard work."

Well, they don't actually ever say exactly that, but that's what writers hear. The thing about these rejections that you need to take to heart and know as truth is that they're not personal even though writers, at least at the start, take them that way. If you take nothing away from this chapter, take this: It's a titanic waste of energy to take rejection personally. The sooner you get there the better.

Producers and managers don't know you. They don't care who you are. It doesn't enter their mind at all. They don't care how hard you worked on your script or how much research you did or the sleepless nights you spent thinking about subplots. How you struggled over every word of dialogue. All they know is the screenplay you've submitted to them. They judge whether they'll be dealing with you on that alone. The rejection isn't of you, it's of what you submitted. Those words on those pages.

When it comes to rejection, producers, agents, managers, or production company execs only know that your script doesn't work for them. They think about your script until they don't have to anymore. Then it's gone. You as a person are not even part of the thought process until they like it and want to talk to you about it.

I once read an internet post by a young woman who talked emotionally about how she'd poured her heart and soul into her first script. How she'd struggled over every single perfect word. And right off the bat, a producer wanted to read it.

To her, it was now a foregone conclusion that this producer would buy and make her screenplay into the film she dreamed about. It was now down to a choice of dresses to wear on the red carpet.

Then the producer got back to her and said, "Pass." Thus, unleashing an onslaught of rage that can only be defined as:

o·ver·re·ac·tion

ˌōvə(r)rēˈakSHən/

noun

a more emotional or forcible response than is justified.

Yep. And after the rage, where she called this producer every word I won't say in this book, she publicly announced she was abandoning her quest to be a screenwriter altogether. She was done. He had unfairly squashed her dreams and kept the world from her amazing script. So, she was taking her ball and going home.

It was sad and unnecessary because rejection is what you should be ready for every day as a screenwriter. It's not something that you want, but you also can't stop it. You can anticipate it, then be surprised when it doesn't happen. That's a lot easier than feeling stomped on every time it does.

I could start a list right now of all the amazing successful scripts that spent years being rejected before someone took a chance on them. Including a couple of mine. But you've read all those stories time and again. Almost every single great script was rejected somewhere, probably many times, before it got picked up and made.

I stopped counting my rejections, my passes, years ago because they got too numerable to count. The first ones are the worst. The one I got last week? Eh. You do get used to them. I'm not sure if that's good or bad, but it's what happens if you do this long enough. Actually, I think I got two last week. Oh well.

I've been at screenwriting social gatherings where writers commiserate over the rejections like they are badges of honor, trading stories about how they were delivered and how many they got that week. It's nothing to be ashamed of or embarrassed about or to feel oppressed by. It's as common to screenwriters as anything they experience.

Screenwriting isn't about anything but the long game. The years of passes before you hear that first yes. All you can do is learn from them, then sluff them off, letting them go. Moving on to the next read. The next submission. The next chance. It's not easy. But better than going crazy.

I feel sorry for that young lady. But if that's how she's going to react to one rejection, she's not ready for number 100. Or number 200. Maybe quitting was the best thing for her. If you can't handle rejection, screenwriting isn't for you.

There are positive aspects to rejection, too. Rejection can be sometimes realizing you need to move on to your next script. That the one you thought was a slam dunk, wasn't exactly what you thought you had. If a series of rejections can give you that realization, you're better off recognizing it and moving to the next one. And the next one. And the next one.

Rejections can force you to relook at your logline to see if it doesn't work and how you can fix it. Or for you to get the idea your query letter is lacking. You have to look at each rejection and the totality of those rejections and see what you can learn from them. There are lessons in everything that happen if you take the time, without ego, to take a close look at them.

They can come in all kinds of packages, too.

PASSES OF ALL SHAPES AND SIZES

Let's talk about each kind of pass you can, and will, get with a little more depth, so you understand what they mean and how to handle them.

The worst is "the silent pass":

When you submit a script and the recipient never gets back to you. Ever. You've waited your three weeks and sent your email reminder and you hear nothing. No email. Nada.

Hate to tell you this, but this is a pass.

Unfortunately, this pass has become the one most used by producers. Where they don't tell you they passed, you're just supposed to assume it. Why would they do this?

A producer once told me they've gone to the silent pass for self-preservation. Too many desperate writers see any kind of response as the opening of a dialogue. These unhappy writers email back, sometimes multiple times, begging or swearing or threatening or arguing or all of these things at once. They can't take no for an answer. It's gotten so bad that the silent pass was born out of it.

Don't think that writers are alone in this kind of pass. It's not new. This is how every actor finds out they didn't get the part they auditioned for. When no one calls. Been that way forever.

If they want your screenplay, they let you know. If not? Radio silence.

The next is the "pass with no explanation." You get an email that says.

```
Dear Writer,

Thank you for your submission. We're
passing on it.

Producers
```

This one is easier to take than the silent pass because you actually get an answer. The answer is no, but it's an answer. You say some choice words to yourself under your breath and save the email to reread to torture yourself for a couple of days before deleting it. Then you get over it. And…

You can respond to it, thusly:

```
Producer/Rep,

Thank you for reading my script. I
appreciate it. Hope we can work together
on another project in the future.

Your Name Here
```

You will be tempted to send something else, don't do it. Don't send anything like this.

Dear Producer or Rep,

Are you crazy? You're making a huge
mistake not buying this script (or
repping me). That script will win an
Oscar one day and you'll be looking at
me giving my acceptance speech never
mentioning you. You are very
shortsighted. But I'm understanding. I'm
going to give you a second chance to
reverse this terrible mistake you've
made.

If not, could you forward me your
extensive notes on the script so I can
rewrite it and resubmit it to you, so we
can get on with our relationship?

If not, I hope all your films (or
clients) fail miserably and you suffer
something horrible personally.

All my best,

Writer

I know on the face of it this looks pretty unbelievable, but
I've talked to producers who get these kinds of messages
after passing on something. Desperate screenwriters send
emails like this all the time and all it does is insure them that
no one affiliated with the producer or rep they sent it to will
ever read anything they write in the future.

I will reiterate this, too, even though it's in the letter. Don't
ask them for notes on improving your script. They may not
have read past page 10, which would be an embarrassing

answer for you to get, and honestly, they have no obligation to give you notes anyway.

People do rash things in the heat of the moment. I get that. One more pass can be a frustrating thing. But please, don't be this desperate. Once you get a pass, they aren't going to change their minds.

Ok.

Next is the most frustrating rejection, the "complimentary" pass.

```
Dear Writer,

Thank you for your delightful script,
"Title Here". We found the writing fresh
and creative. It was a pleasure to read.
We're passing on it.

Producers
```

Yeah, I don't get it either. It's like the first three sentences are supposed to soften the blow. They don't. What you can't do is get all excited that they liked it. They didn't. Otherwise they would have optioned it. They also didn't ask what else you had. Another clue that they really didn't care for it.

These kinds of passes are deceptive, and you can't take them for anything but a really nice pass. Send a thank you for reading response and move on.

Then there's the "We already have something like it in development" pass. You don't need to see that letter because this is all it says before they say, "Pass". This pass is also frustrating because if they aren't lying to you, somebody thought of your idea before you did and did it well enough to have them option it. This happens all the time. Statistically, it pretty much has to do with so many scripts out there. Congratulate yourself for having a saleable idea and query it to someone else.

Finally, the "It's not for us, but what else do you have" pass. This says it all. Then, you need to pick your next best script and send it with a "Thank you for requesting this new script" email. And you wait again. This pass is rare and very good because they liked the way you write enough to ask for another script.

You will also get passes on your optioned scripts.

You can get an email or call about your script that has been optioned and re-optioned for the last three years from a producer who says, "We tried. Just couldn't get it made." Another rejection. You thank them for believing in it, hope you can work together on something else in the future, and go about doing a rewrite/polish on the same script so you can get it back out there again.

The funny thing is, my wife takes these rejections way more personally than I do, which I appreciate. She gets incensed, then annoyed at me because I tell her it's not personal.

I know a very prominent screenwriter. Well known and well liked in the industry. Multiple screenwriting credits on well-known films. He recently wrote his first original spec in years and was extremely excited about it. He had his reps send it out to everyone and, all passes. Everywhere. It's dead for now. It happens to every writer, successful or not. His quote, "Oh well."

So, gird your loins and get ready for rejection. It's going to be a big part of your life if you want to be a screenwriter. Learn from it, then let it go. It makes life a lot easier if you do.

CHAPTER 15

DEVELOPMENT

Congratulations! You optioned your script to a producer or production company. Break out the champagne. It's worthy of celebration.

But not too much. There's still a whole lot more work to be done.

If you're the one who gets to do it. More on that later.

For this exercise, let's say you get to be the one who does the development writing for the next draft of the script.

Huh? Next draft? Bob, thought when they option it, they try to get financing for the script and maybe attach a director and actors? Don't they just use my script to do that?

You have a lot to learn. Let's start now.

NOTES

Welcome to the real world of screenwriting. Nothing I have said so far will come close to preparing you for what comes after you option your script.

Right after your contract is signed, you will get notes on your script.

I'm going to give you a quick lesson on how much control you have over your script once you option or sell it, using your car. If you sell your car, take money for it and hand the buyer the pink slip, that buyer gets to take that car and paint flames on it if they want to. You have no power to stop them.

When you sell, or even option a script, it's just like that car. If producers want to paint flames on it, you have zero say about it. The way they paint those flames is with "notes."

Let's define what notes are first.

For the people who aren't writers and read this, notes are the mandatory, unless you can logically talk them out of some, changes to your script that you get from producers, directors, development execs, the guy who waters the plants at the production office, actors, distributors, studio execs, network execs, and anyone else you can think of that might come in contact with your script during development or pre-production.

Notes you can get at every stage of production. Notes you can get up to and including the day that a particular scene gets shot.

They can be as small as a change of one word in a sentence of dialogue to changing the entire story. Not part of the entire story. The entire story. And anything you can think of in between.

They can come in a production meeting where a group of the people involved sit around a conference table and tell you what you need to change in your script.

They will all be talking to you. You need to be ready.

Or notes can come in a long, involved email, from an individual producer, sometimes pages and pages of notes. But mostly you meet in an office someplace that you have to pay your own way to get to. You pay for your hotel, too, if you're coming in from out of town. Sometimes they understand you have to travel and will hold the meeting on a conference call. My advice to you is to get yourself to the office in person for at least the first meeting so they have a face to put with the name. If they meet you and interact with you face to face it's much better for you. It's easier for them to fire someone they've never met in person.

You'll be nervous and scared. This is natural. You also need to not show it. Then, they'll hit you with their changes.

For some writers this is a hard thing to take. Changes to their baby. To take something they worked tirelessly on for months to years to create and then have to throw out or change huge portions of it to fit what the people paying for it want. You can't be the writer who thinks that their work is untouchable. You can't be hurt or mad or anything emotional. You get emotional, you lose, big time.

When I was first starting out, I felt that way. My script was perfect the way it was and shouldn't be touched. I learned fast you can't think like that. If you do, they'll smile and have their first meeting with you and then call you a few days later and fire you. From the film of your own original screenplay.

Your script is going to change whether you do the work or not. The only way it will stay the way you wrote it is if you put up the money to produce it yourself or lock it in a drawer and never have it see the light of day.

Every script gets changed. Every one of them. And they all get changed in significant ways. They get changed on independent films, they get changed on cable movies, they get changed on production company films, they get changed on studio films.

Even if you're a writer/director, if there are finance people, producers, distributors, actors? You will have to change your script to satisfy those people. Maybe not as much, but enough to make a difference from the original.

Your script will never be seen on the screen the way you wrote it, if you option or sell it. It just won't. In fact, not one single word you wrote might end up on the screen. It happens.

I know this is tough to see and tougher to wrap your head around, but it's the nature of the film business.

You will sit in shock as you get notes to change your main character completely. Maybe change him to a her. Maybe change their personality completely. Maybe change their profession. Change their marital status. Change their entire motivation in the story. Maybe get rid of that character completely in favor of another one you didn't even write.

Or change your story completely. The plot. The setting. The characters. Everything but the premise, which they'll fool with, too.

This happens in some form with every script.

I've been on both sides of notes. Getting notes on my scripts and giving them on scripts I didn't write, but would like to rewrite and get paid for. The giving part usually happens when a production company contacts me and wants me to read a script they've bought or optioned and want me to give them my opinion on it. This also happens, most of the time, after the original writer has been given a chance to implement their notes, but can't or won't change it the way they want.

When I get a script to rewrite, I get notes from the development execs and the producers to start. They're usually very general and sweeping, otherwise they wouldn't be hiring me. I do, mostly, what are called "page one rewrites" where I usually take the original author's script and change it so much it's unrecognizable to them.

You're thinking right now, *What?*

I don't do this lightly and I always feel badly for the original author, who I never speak to during this process, but, those writers, most of the time, have had their chance to do this and wouldn't or couldn't. Plus, they're still going to get a screen credit, if they were smart enough to put it in their contract if it was non-union, and by now have been paid. Unless it's an option, where you don't get paid until the first day of production.

Wait? They do this to my script when it's just optioned? While it's rented? They haven't even bought it yet?

Yep. They're trying to attract money and a director and stars. This is what they think will do it. What you think doesn't matter. Get used to this.

There's more.

They can also change every character name. The title. All your plot points. Your inciting incident. The locations.

Everything.

I've had to rewrite my original scripts. Some more than others. A couple of times making them almost unrecognizable to me, and I did the rewrite.

Did some of the notes I got make my scripts better?

In most cases, I have to be honest and say they did. Some notes made a few of them much better. In one case, they made the script so much better I'm grateful to have worked with this director and hope I can again.

Hold on, Bob. They made your script better? Really?

Now, I get to talk about how creative, savvy, and intelligent most producers, production execs, and directors are. At least the ones I've worked with and I've worked with quite a few. These people aren't in these positions by accident and people aren't financing their films to the tune of millions of dollars because they don't know what they're doing. They mostly do. You can learn a whole lot from these people if you pay attention.

You hear on social media how awful producers are. How they'll ruin your script. Or that directors will throw out your vision of the story and substitute their own. How you'll be treated like scum by these people.

That hasn't been my experience. Yes, there have been difficult times. Yes, I have been fired off of projects and other writers brought in after me. But that happens on just about every film to every writer. It's rare when there's only one or two writers.

But these filmmakers, these producers and directors, don't want to ruin your script. They're doing what they think will make the best, most profitable film out of your screenplay. They saw the value of it, otherwise they wouldn't be trying to make it. This is something you need to understand to survive as a screenwriter.

Honestly, they can and will make your script better in a lot of cases, even if they want huge fundamental changes to it. They have the experience to know what works, what attracts the actors they want, the director they'd like to have. They've done this before.

These production execs are not your enemy. It's not an adversarial relationship unless you choose to make it one. Then, they fire you and hire me, who knows it's not adversarial.

It's never personal. It's strictly about the material. Problem is, the material is personal to you. So, it's very hard sometimes. You have to hang in and remember your goal, a produced film with your name on it. That always made getting notes easier for me.

How you respond to notes will have a great deal of influence on your career and maybe if you'll have one at all.

So, heading into any notes meeting, you need to mentally set yourself before you go in. Know ahead of time the notes may not be what you want to hear, but that you need to actively work to be acceptive and take them seriously.

When you're in there, pay attention, write everything down you can, be open minded, and not instantly reactive. Give yourself time to think about each note. I know when I do that, after some serious thought, I can often see how to use them to make the script better. Even notes I hated on first take.

Then, if you truly hate some of them, logically and gently fight for them not to be used. No emotion. You can't ever win with emotion.

One way to do this is to know your script and story and characters so well that you can intelligently and calmly explain why some notes will not work if they want to keep the story you wrote. You have to know every motivation. Every little thing about your characters. What they would do and wouldn't do in any situation. Be ready to back up your research.

Remember the "ripple effect"? You explain, from your thorough knowledge of your script and story, one change they want will have a ripple effect on the whole script, changing things they may not want changed. I use that all the time. They respond well to it because it makes sense and is logical. Or you can explain that the characters wouldn't do the thing they want and how it would negatively affect the audience's perception of the character.

You really do have to know your script inside and out, so you can rationally explain these things. This does work because I've done it time and again and, more often than not, have won those arguments.

But, if they say, "Thank you for your knowledgeable measured response, but change it anyway," that's what you do, the best way you can.

It's up to you to implement the notes, even if it hurts. You, as the writer, are one cog in a huge machine that is film and TV. You cooperate to the optimum of your ability and do the best job you can making the script the way they've asked for it to be, and they will start to trust you. If they trust you, they might start asking you for your opinion on elements of the film that may not even have to do with your job. It's happened to me. You also have a better chance of being on set when it gets shot.

So how do I do this? What's my personal way of implementing notes?

I take their general notes, combined with the notes I gave on the script that the producers liked, and I write a draft. I get rid of the things they wanted gone. I change the things they wanted, but I do it my way. Not necessarily exactly the way they wanted. I let myself be creative within the spirit of their notes. And I always save the previous draft, because they'll sometimes recognize they need some of the stuff they cut or changed back to the way it was before.

Again, they want the best film they can make from their vision of it. They don't do things purposefully to hurt those chances. They will put things back or change things back if they recognize they need to. You just have to hang in there long enough to be the one who puts them back.

Then I write another draft based on more of their notes after they read the first rewrite. Then another draft with more notes. Then if they don't give it to another writer to rewrite again, I do a polish. Or rewrite it again.

Then the director might do his own draft or give me more notes to change it again to fit his/her vision. Then maybe another polish. Then a production draft, then, you get the drift. Sometimes, any remote resemblance to the original script is a miracle. Sometimes, they've gone full circle back to something close to what you sold them. Jeff Willis and I did seven drafts of *The Right Girl* for the producers before we got to a shooting script.

This is what development is.

The first few couple of times you have to do this will be the hardest. As you do it more, you get a feel for what has to happen for a film to get made and you'll get used to and understand being part of a team. This team is what gets films made.

I wish I could tell you there was one tried and true way to handle notes. Each piece of the notes puzzle is different every time you do it. Producers, production execs, actors, directors. It's individual to that project. Each of those creatives have different expectations of the writer each time and you have to learn to adapt to what they want for that individual project. It's those writers that do who have long careers.

Every time *Extracurricular Activities* was optioned, and it got optioned a lot, the notes were different because the producers were different and had different visions and goals for the film. In some cases, vastly different from the ones I got from the producers and the director who finally made the film. I was extremely fortunate those men had close to the same vision I did when I wrote it, because my story remained pretty intact in their version. Not completely, but close enough for me.

That happens. On some projects they can use a substantial amount of your script, or circle back around to it. They will change parts of it for sure, but at least you recognize it. It's the luck of the draw and, honestly, how great your script is to begin with. Like I said, there are very few great scripts.

Some of my films are pretty close to what I wrote in their final shooting draft and I was happy with them. Some aren't close. One film with my name on it hasn't got a single word I wrote on screen, because it was rewritten by the director after I was off the project. Why was my name on it? It was in my contract. And trust me on this, any credit is a good credit.

Ok. What about if they can't get the financing and my option lapses? What happens to my script, Bob?

You get your original script back. Exactly the way they bought it.

Ok, good. But what about the notes I liked. The ones that made it better? I can use those, right?

Wrong. You can't use those notes. You don't own them. They own them. Their ideas. They gave them to you to use on a script they wanted changed to make their way. If you use them after your option lapses, they can claim at a later date they own a piece of the script, which can screw up another deal you might have.

This happens all the time. So, you have to be smart and careful.

You can try to put in your contract that you own all the notes if they don't make it and you get your script back, but that rarely works and can be a deal killer for them. Doesn't hurt to try though. Out of a few dozen or so contracts, I've gotten it in my contracts twice, I think.

If you get your script back from an option, you give it a polish and get it back out there to option again. If you do option it again, you wait for the notes from those new producers. If they give you the same great notes you got before, keep good records of that correspondence, and you're ok. But you can't use those notes yourself unless you want some trouble down the line.

I know this sounds complicated, but navigating notes is complicated and a big part of the job.

As a screenwriter, the sooner you realize that script notes are integral, whether given to you or coming from you, and you realize it's up to you to be cooperative and innovative in seeing those notes through to the best of your ability, the sooner you are going to be recognized as a pro.

CHAPTER 16

SCREENWRITING AS A BUSINESS

You've written your script. You're querying. You're networking. You're doing anything you can to get your scripts out there that's not illegal, immoral, or stupid. Is that it?

Your job as a screenwriter has other requirements beyond writing and marketing. You also need to be armed with knowledge about the industry you want to be a part of. You'll notice I used the word "Industry", not the words "Artistic Endeavor".

Industry. Business.

If you want to be a screenwriter and you want to succeed, you need to absolutely understand the business end of things.

Yes, films and TV can be art, but that art is a byproduct of the business that brought it into being. Film and TV is nothing but a big business. Just like any other big business.

I spent the first 20 years of my working life in the wholesale furniture industry. A billion-dollar industry. I was deeply involved in the business end of it. I'm often asked what the difference is between the furniture industry and the film business. My answer every time?

Nothing. Not a thing.

They're huge businesses that have different products. They operate in the same ways. The people who run them do so with their eyes on the bottom line and on which new products they can make that will enhance that bottom line further.

When a producer or production company options or buys a script from you, it's a business decision, not an artistic one. They think your script can enhance their bottom line. You, as a writer, can never forget this. Never forget that at the end of the day, you're involved in a business.

You need to be thinking about your business as a screenwriter from the start. By the time you get an option or a write for hire job, you'd better be in that mindset or you won't last a week. You need to look at every interaction and communication with producers and reps through a business lens.

A screenwriter once touched base with me with a question. She had a script that a producer said she loved. Loved. The producer would like to option it and move forward, but, she was too busy with other projects to take it on right now.

My immediate thought was, "This is the nicest pass ever." Not fair to the writer, but a still a pass. Yes, you got it, the dreaded complimentary pass.

Why did I think that? Because I think that anytime they don't actually give you a contract to sign, it's a 100% pass.

You should think that, too. It will save you a lot of grief. If that producer really wanted the script, she would have optioned it.

That said, the writer in question said the producer left her with the impression that she would come back at an unspecified later date and option the script from her. So, for the point of this exercise, we're going to buy this.

Her question was, "Should I put my script away and wait for her to come back to me?" My well thought out answer was instant. "Are you out of your mind?" No. Double no. And if that wasn't clear enough. NO!

Here's where I go to my car example again. You own a car. You want to sell it. A buyer comes and says, "I love this car and I think I'd like to buy it, but I'm busy for the next six months, so if you don't show it to anyone in that time and save it for me, maybe I'll come back and buy it. But don't contact me or ask about it."

Are you gonna put that car in the garage and forget about selling it and wait for that buyer? Only if you're not thinking like a businessperson.

You, as a writer and businessperson, need to do what's best for you and your business. Your bottom line. That means you get that script right back out there to option or sell and if this producer wants to buy it at a later date, she has to take her chances it's still available.

You certainly don't put it away in hopes the producer might come back. I can promise you that same producer wouldn't do anything close to this for you. No producer would.

Screenwriters sometimes forget that they are like any other business trying to sell a commodity. You built/created something and now you want to sell it. Build and sell. That's the whole idea, unless you want to make it yourself.

You own a business. You network to sell yourself as a writer and your scripts. You query. You work to get a manager or agent. You enter contests. You network more.

To sell your product.

Not to give it away or take a bad deal because you're desperate to have anyone make your script into a film or TV show at any cost.

Without a business mindset, you're a pigeon, waiting to be plucked by people in this industry who would love for all writers to think they are betting from a weaker hand. They love writers who come to them thinking they're in a perpetual subservient position in any negotiation or deal and should be grateful for anything they get. This happens all the time to writers who are fearful and desperate and buy this hogwash.

These are the same writers who don't realize that they need to treat their work like a business and deal with it that way. The same writers who wonder what happened when they get taken advantage of.

If you're a good writer, you possess a valuable skill. If everyone could do it, there wouldn't be a demand for good writers. There is. Good writers who understand what they have.

Be confident in yourself and your business. If you have producers who want to talk to you about your work, it's because they see value in it. Those producers think you belong in that room with them. You need to believe the same thing, not dealing from a weakened position because you're fearful of them.

I'm not saying you make demands that are unreasonable, but you act like you belong there and you're ready to conduct fair and equitable business with them. Without the emotion that often gets in the way.

This goes for agents and managers, too. There is no need to feel you're in a weak position when dealing with them either. As a writer you'd don't work for a manager or an agent, you work with them, like a business partnership.

It takes a while for most writers to get to this place. Every successful writer is there. Every one of them. They know their business is to think of great stories and write them down. A semi-rare commodity. One that is valued.

If you don't think that way, start to. Learn to value yourself and what you have and treat your writing as a business. Your fear and desperation will vanish.

<u>YOUR BUSINESS</u>

Like any business, you need to keep good records.

Records of who you queried and when. I have friends who use Excel to do that. They set up their own system. Whatever works for you. But the last thing you want to do is query the same producer two or three times with the same script because you didn't keep records.

This way you can track who, when, and what the response was, if there was a response, and when you followed up.

You keep track of requested scripts, when you sent them and when you followed up and what the end status was.

You keep track of option dates and option expiration dates, and money collected for those options. That money needs to be declared as income.

You open a business file on your computer and put every contract, message, communication, or document from every project in it, back them up on another drive, then print out paper copies and file those, if you want to. At some point you'll need one of them and it's nice to be able to put your hands on them instantly. Or just put your hands on them, period. Not being able to do that can cost you money.

I have a huge file on my computer that's called BobBusiness. It's loaded with everything from my contracts, addendums to contracts, call sheets, my headshots, my loglines for unsold scripts, movie posters from my films, 25, 50, 100, and 250-word prewritten bios, so I have them when they're requested. Script notes on produced films I worked on from directors, from producers, from actors. My resume. Business tax info. Every scrap of paper for every project I've ever worked on. All that I can get to if I have to, and it's backed up in two places.

Keep the industry business cards you've collected networking in some kind of order and in a safe place. You'll be surprised when they come in handy even if you keep those numbers on your phone.

You track your expenses. What you've paid out building your business.

Screenwriting software. Books. Research costs. Traveling anywhere. Trips to LA for producer or production meetings.

Writing conferences. Hotels for any of them. Airfare. Rental cars. Or if you use your own car, the mileage. Business cards. Paid script placement sites. Paid pitchfests. Paid industry websites. This list goes on...

You need to check with your own tax preparer as to what you individually can deduct, but those are legitimate costs of doing your business and you need to keep good records of them.

Keep your original paper copyrights all together in one place but also scan them all into a separate folder, so you have them whenever you need them in more than one place.

Not only will this record keeping help you find documentation when you need to, but will put you in more of a business mode yourself.

BUSINESS CARDS

Yes, you should have one. A lot of them will get thrown away or forgotten on desks or in drawers, but it only takes one person who really intends to get back to you to make them a valuable thing to have.

This should seem logical, but I'm going to talk about what you should have on your card, and shouldn't have on it.

On your card? Your name. Your cell number. Your email address. You can put "Writer" or "Screenwriter" under your name. Mine just says "Writer" and only to remind them why they asked for the card.

About your email address? It needs to be professional. It needs to be your name or as close to your name as possible. I know a producer who took a card from someone she was interested in, saw the writer's email was BabyPrincess12@email.com or something like it, and threw the card away. I watched her do it. I asked her why. She said, "That tells me they won't be professional." I know that seems unfair, but it really happened.

I've also met new writers with emails like BestScreenwriterEver@ or AmazingScripts@ or, you get the idea. These are instant turnoffs to producers and reps.

You can keep and use those for personal use if you want, but for your professional life you need a professional email.

When you get a rep, you put their name and number on the business card, too.

That's it. That's your card. Simple. Businesslike.

CONSPIRACY THEORIES

Part of understanding this business is understanding it's not stacked against you, either. That Hollywood is not a closed shop that keeps new writers out.

Here's something you really need to know.

There is no Hollywood.

None. It doesn't exist except in the minds of people who've bought the whole Hollywood Mystique. It's a bunch of separate companies, studios, and producers that couldn't all agree on any rules if they wanted to, and they don't.

Each one sets their own policies on how they do business. I've dealt with quite a few of them and they are all unique and all have approaches to this business that differs company to company, producer to producer, manager to manager.

So, stop now with any thought that there's some big entity called Hollywood.

But Bob, what about the Hollywood conspiracy against new writers? An organized effort to thwart new writers from breaking in? It seems like a closed industry dedicated to keeping new writers out. How is that a fair business?

I know this is a question every writer has asked themselves. Well, every writer except me and a few thousand other relatively sane writers who have a reasonable grasp on reality.

Like there is no Hollywood, there is no conspiracy. No cabal of producers who sit and twirl their mustaches and plot to keep spec scripts from being read or optioned. People who want to keep the industry closed to new ideas or new writers. Why would any business handicap themselves like this? They wouldn't. Yes, the industry is hard to break into. But any big industry is hard to break into. It takes work and perseverance and patience.

You mean I have to pay my dues? I don't get what I want because I want it? Now? Then there must be a conspiracy.

At a writers' board I lurk on sometimes to see what people are asking and thinking about this business, I was not surprised to see the often-asked question, "Why won't Hollywood just open its doors for new writers?" "Why do they keep making the same films all the time?" "Why don't they buy spec scripts?" or, "Why don't they buy *my* spec script?"

Because they don't operate their businesses that way. And they want your new script, if it's great. You have to do the work through their channels to do it.

As for most specs? I'll tell you why they don't buy those specs. They probably aren't ready to be seen. They were probably queried or networked to get them read before they were ready or was written about a subject matter no one wants to buy. Or doesn't have a compelling story. Tough words, but those are the main reasons why spec scripts don't get optioned or sell.

I have seen real anger from people who can't believe their script, usually their first script, isn't the toast of Hollywood immediately upon its completion. I mean, sometimes it's pure rage. I often see posts from writers who say, "Hollywood needs to be changed. I say we writers band together and change it." and I ask them, "How would you change it?"

They say 100% of the time, "Open it up to everybody. Have the studios stop making remakes and sequels and superhero movies and start buying specs again and make original films."

I point out that the studios make these kinds of films because they're profitable, there's a demand and an audience for them, and, they are corporations who get to make what they want no matter how many writers band together.

They are not in business to make things easier for *you*.

Like I said, producers love new writers who can deliver. They also know that they're uncommon.

I have a friend who's a reader for a big production house. Big. She once told me that over a three month period she recommended one script and read well over a hundred and she's a good reader. In the past year I've read three scripts I thought were great, out of the close to a hundred I've read. two of them were from previously optioned writers. It's not easy. You can do it though.

The angry writers say to this, "Then why is there so much crap made?" Well, first of all, crap is in the eye of the beholder. Lots of what you may think of as crap has an audience and makes money and that's the whole idea of the film business. The rest of it? I've seen great scripts turned into not great films over and over again.

But they were great scripts to begin with.

It's easy for me to say, "Just write a great script". It's much, much harder to do. Those great scripts you've read? They didn't just appear. The hours and days and months and years of extremely hard work to get there aren't charted on the cover page, but you can see it in the content.

No one is trying to keep you from succeeding. The competition is ferocious for sure. But great scripts with great ideas do rise to the top. They don't always get made, but they do rise and get noticed. The writers who can consistently deliver on the promise of that great script get to make a living writing for films and TV.

But there's no conspiracy.

FAME & RESPECT

I'm sure you've heard over and over from other writers, blogs, the internet, that screenwriters don't get any respect from the rest of the film business.

Here's the thing. Writers respect writers. Directors, for the most part, respect writers. Producers love and respect good cooperative creative writers, know who they are, and remember them. Production executives like and appreciate writers who know what they're doing. They all also know and understand the necessity of the writer. Industry people from all walks pay attention to who writes what. They know. Serious film buffs know who some writers are, especially the A-list ones.

A small percentage of the public will see something based on who wrote it. By small, I mean very very small, bordering on microscopic, when you take the whole population into consideration.

The public at large?

Not so much. They know somebody probably wrote the films they see, but man, did you see those dinosaurs? Or that explosion? Or how the actors in that scene made you cry? Or how cool the film looked? Or that car they drove out of that plane?

They do notice writers when the film sucks. "Who wrote that crap?" But even then, they don't actually look and see who did.

On the films or TV they loved and were entertained? Don't kid yourself. They may look at the name, but it's gone by the time they get home or go to bed.

But Bob, there are screenwriting podcasts. And books. And websites. And seminars. And blogs. You're selling a book about it. It's a big business, screenwriting. You said so yourself.

It is. For screenwriters or people who would like to be screenwriters.

So, why doesn't the public care who the writers are?

How do I count the ways? Writers are invisible. You never see them onscreen. Their names are on the film once, as the audience is walking in or walking out. The audience didn't come to see the writer. They may have come to see the story the writer created, but they never consider who wrote it. Or they go to see the stars, or the hype. The writer is never on late night talk shows to promote the film. You never see the writer walk the red carpet either. They do walk it, but when that happens, it's time to cut to commercial.

Writers do get to be on panels at film festivals, but those are for the small percentage of people who actually care who the writer is and want to hear from them and mostly it's people who want to be writers, too.

Do I sound bitter? Absolutely not. I started out as an actor. When I decided to try writing, I knew what the bottom line was. I knew where the writer was on the public's food chain. I knew if I succeeded, I would have to be content having the industry know who I was as a pinnacle. I'm still working there.

You don't get into the screenwriting business to get famous. I got into it because I wasn't that good an actor so I thought I'd try it because I love movies and making movies and don't want to do anything else. What I found out was that I loved writing. I loved creating story. I loved fitting all the story elements together like puzzle pieces. And the first time I saw my script, my story, my characters, my dialogue on a screen, I was hooked. A junkie. I want it again and again and again.

Everyone has their own reasons why they write for film or TV. Getting famous shouldn't be one of them. Being famous isn't all it's cracked up to be anyway. I've been out to dinner, played golf, and had drinks with some very famous people and I wouldn't want that kind of public attention for anything. It might be fun for a while, but for me it would wear very thin.

So, for that group of writers, or would be writers out there who think it's not fair that writers aren't as publicly valued as actors and directors,

Don't blame the industry.

It's the public. They're the ones that don't care. They just want to be entertained and thrilled or to laugh or cry or be frightened. No more. No less. And if you as a writer can accomplish that and can sit in the theater or in a home or in a screening room with people watching something you wrote and they react to your work in any of those ways, you've gotten everything you need from them.

You don't need to be stopped in the grocery store or walking your dog for autographs because, well, it's not going to happen.

And, to be honest, I've also noticed that most of the people who complain the loudest about no public recognition of screenwriters are the ones who've never sold anything or had anything produced.

Having the respect of industry peers beats the heck out of anyone recognizing you in Costco anyway.

MAKING A LIVING AS A SCREENWRITER

Knowing when to quit your day job and do this full time is a very serious decision, complicated by responsibilities, family, debt, you name it.

As I have said repeatedly in this book so far, success as a screenwriter takes years and continued success isn't guaranteed in any way. Just like there are one hit wonders in the music business, the one hit wonder is a part of the screenwriting world, too.

I've listened as screenwriters complained that they got one script sold expecting the whole film industry to take notice and make them a household name, and…

then, nothing.

Continued success is as hard to attain as your first option or sale. There are so many factors in place. Your attitude working with producers and directors. Your skill taking and implementing notes. Your knowledge about how films actually get made…

The list is long and the road bumpy.

But, you can do it. Deciding when to make the full time move? All I can give you is my best advice.

After you've sold a script and it got made, with some success, and have gotten writing assignments with more than a couple of producers and production companies and made some good money?

Maybe do it full time.

It's much better to be established longer before you make that kind of move than to do it too early and starve. Or be forced to ask for your old job back. The first time you sell a script you'll be tempted to quit your job and tell them you're a screenwriter now. Resist this temptation. Especially if you have a family looking at you for support.

The percentage of people screenwriting full time is small compared to the people with scripts out there.

When you think the time is right, wait for one more great job, then make the move. Not before. You'll thank me for this.

WRITING AND MARKETING OUTSIDE OF LA / MOVING TO LA

I get asked this question all the time. "Do I need to be in Hollywood to sell a script or be a screenwriter?"

No, you don't and Yes, you do.

For films, producers don't care where you live if they love the script. It's the script that matters and they can option your script no matter where you live. You can do rewrites from where you live, too.

At some point, if you want to be involved with your project beyond selling it, get more work, and have them know you, you will have to go see them at some point.

I get asked this when the subject of travelling to LA comes up, "If they option your script, do they pay your way to LA and pay for your hotel?"

I covered this earlier, but I'll repeat it. The answer to this is a resounding NO. They do not. This is where I remind you again that it's a business and you are an independent contractor. The cost of going to LA is completely yours as a writer. It's not cheap. Yes, there are exceptions, but they are few and those writers earned it.

I don't live in LA. I live 400 or so miles away. I have to go to LA quite a bit during the year for all kinds of meetings and I pay my own deductible expenses. So does every other writer who lives somewhere else if they want to go to LA.

If you want to write for TV, that's where the YES answer comes in. No matter where they film most shows, the writer's rooms are almost all in LA. If you want to be a TV writer, you need to be there.

LA is one of the most expensive areas in the country. No matter how much you think it will cost, the reality will be a lot more. You pretty much have to have a car, although I know people who get around without them using rideshare companies, but that's expensive, too.

I've known writers who moved to LA with a few thousand dollars, giving themselves six months to "make it". Were they sure they'd be successful and working as a screenwriter in six months? You bet they were. Were they living in a rainbow unicorn dream induced state? You bet they were. Were they warned? You bet they were. Did they come anyway and make it in six months? No. Why? Because that's not the way it works.

You don't make the move to LA until you've been able to support yourself with writing or you have a ton of money in the bank to support yourself or you're willing to work a day job or two to pay the bills while you're working on your writing career. Either way, you don't come without having made solid contacts or gotten representation through querying, options, and networking. Moving to LA not knowing anyone and without any professional contacts is a guarantee of moving back home within a year or two and having to explain to your friends that it wasn't what you thought.

It's easier if you're young and single without a lot of debt, but you'll still need money. So, lining up a day job before you arrive is probably a good idea.

If you have a family? You especially don't uproot your family and move there without a great job lined up or a solid track record of screenwriting success, like I said above.

I know LA seems like a mystical place where producers and agents are in every bar and restaurant taking numbers to meet everyone who comes into town, but that's not the case. Coming to LA is a huge step that shouldn't be taken lightly or done gambling on incredible luck.

Stay where you are and write. You can succeed from there to start. Your address isn't on your title page, with the advent of cell phones every area code lives in LA, and emails don't say where they originated. No one knows where you are until it becomes necessary to say anything about it.

And when the time is right and you want to, then you make that move.

Until then, you owe it to yourself to be as thoughtful and careful as you can before making that kind of monumental decision.

One more thing…

THE ONE THING HOLLYWOOD HATES THE MOST: DESPERATION

Here's my conundrum. Do I be blunt about how bad it is to be a desperate screenwriter or do I soft pedal it? Make it more palatable for you to understand. The problem is that being desperate for success, for people to read your work, to meet industry people, it all affects the way you're perceived by those people you want so desperately to impress.

What's wrong with being desperate?

Desperate people do, say, try, and think stupid things. For a certain percentage of writers, logic and thought go right out the door when it comes to their scripts.

I understand how much work it takes to write and finish a script. Well, most scripts. I read one a while back that the writer bragged he'd written in two days; 144 pages. It just came as a "stream of thought and is destined to be a hit." All you can do with writers like this is smile, point, and say "Look, a producer," and run away when they turn their head.

It takes a ton of work to finish a script. When you're done, it's your new baby. You love it and will do anything to protect it and get it seen, even if you can't realize it may be ugly.

One my dearest friends is an exec at a prominent production company. To say he's bombarded daily with read requests is a gross understatement. Most of the time he rightly says, "No." That can be based on many things. His time and his interest in the logline. Sometimes he reads things as a favor to someone.

When he does consent to read a script, he's very clear that it's not in any way shape or form an acceptance to buy or consider that script for his company. He's in no position at that particular company to bring in outside work.

So, when all he can do to help them is give them some notes and advice on their script, some act like he's gone back on his word to them. He's likely to hear either anger that he doesn't know a good script when he reads it, how wrong he is, sob stories, begging, rage, insults, threats, and other acts of desperation that insure to these writers that my friend and his company will be ignoring them for now and evermore.

I understand desperation. I understand waiting for an email or waiting by the phone for a call. As an actor, I'd audition for some film or commercial or TV show, desperate for the job, then go home and worry and fret in desperation to hear if I got it. I didn't get those parts and I finally figured out why. Desperation shows on camera and casting people and producers and directors hate it.

I had to fight not to be desperate. It's a natural emotion when you really want something. But you have to fight it because it's self-destructive.

I had to learn not to do it as a writer, too. Desperation shows. It shows in your attitude. It shows in your query letters if you're not careful and smart. It shows when you try to network. Bugging people and refusing to take no for an answer is the ultimate act of desperation and makes you look crazy and no one wants to work with crazy.

Don't get me wrong, it's hard not to be desperate in certain situations. I get that. But you can't act like it or show it. It will affect outcomes and relationships. It can kill some relationships before they have a chance to start.

It's just plain hard to option or sell a movie script or TV show. It's really, really hard. It gets harder if you're desperate.

REMEMBER

You want to be thought of as professional from the beginning of your voyage as a screenwriter. It gives you a head start over those who still cling to the magical thinking a lot of new screenwriters imagine is the way the industry really operates.

It operates as a business. You treat it that way, treat your own business that way, and the chances of you taking something to the bank from it increases.

CHAPTER 17

FILM ASSIGNMENT WRITING

If you want to have a full-time career as a screenwriter, you need to know you probably won't be able to live off of spec script sales alone. They are so few and far between and, truthfully, rare these days that you can't make any kind of living from those sales alone.

Unless you want to be a TV writer in a series writing room, which are the most competitive jobs in writing, and you have to be in LA for, and have some kind of track record of success with, you need to look elsewhere for income.

Professional screenwriters know this and that's why they pursue assignment work. They know that 90% of all screenwriting income comes from assignment work.

Rewrite jobs.

Book adaptations.

Writing for hire.

It's been about that percentage for me, too.

So, if you want to do this you need to learn about these kinds of jobs and what they encompass. So, if after you've written that one great script and gotten some meetings and attention, which is how I got my first assignment work, or you've optioned a script and they loved your attitude and saw your skill as someone who can deal with notes and implement them, you might be offered a chance at one of these OWAs.

OWA? Open. Writing. Assignments.

<u>REWRITE JOBS</u>

These jobs entail you rewriting someone else's script for producers who have either optioned or purchased that screenplay. It's your job, as someone who doesn't have an emotional attachment to the script, to rewrite it into what the producers or director want in order to get financing to make it, or to be what they want to shoot, if the financing is in place.

You'll be given the script to read, first. Before they send it, I always ask them the same question, "Why did you option or buy this script?" Their answer will tell me what to look for as I read the script. Did they buy it just for the premise? Did they like the approach to the story the original writer took? Did they buy it because one character is great? Did they buy it for the ending? Did they buy it for, any number of reasons? I need to know why, so my personal notes to them will reflect that.

Then, I read it once on my iPad in one sitting to get a feel for it. Just looking at, or in some cases, for, the story. What's missing? What are the major plot holes? What, overall in the story, does and doesn't make sense? What works?

I make some general notes on my trusty yellow legal pad.

Then I print the script out and go page by page, looking at the scenes. Do they advance the story or not? I look at the characters. Are they consistent, are they unique? The dialogue, is it real or on the nose? The subtext, the subplots, and I red pen the heck out of it, based on what they told me as to why they bought it and my own critique of the script.

Then back to the yellow legal pad. I make more notes, on what my personal approach to rewriting this story will be.

If I think it's a page one rewrite or not.

You won't like being on the other side of a page one rewrite as the original writer. But for the hired writer it's a huge challenge. To keep the intentions of the original writer, think about what it was that producers bought it for, and rebuild it from the ground up in four to six weeks.

A page one rewrite is a complete rewrite of the story, top to bottom. Usually, very little of what was in the original script remains when a page one rewrite is complete. The premise. The protagonist. Maybe the same antagonist, maybe not. Some scenes, completely rewritten, but still there, a few lines of dialogue might be left, but not much more.

Between your notes and extensive notes from producers, you have a pretty good roadmap of where you need to take the script. You can't even think about how it affects what the original script was or the person who wrote it.

If you find that depressing for the original writer, I get it. I always feel a twinge of empathy for them. I know how they feel. Been done to me. But someone is going to do this rewrite and, to be honest, I'd rather it was me. Just as you'd rather it was you getting a job like this. Once it's been decided to do this to a script, there's no going back to the original. This rewrite is a forgone conclusion for the producers once they make up their minds they want it. They just need to find the right writer.

Sometimes, you'll do all this work and give them your notes and don't get the job because they have 10 other writers doing the same thing and are going to pick the one whose notes they like best, combined with their experience and writing voice for this particular job.

If you get the job, you get a contract, you negotiate pay, you have a meeting of some kind with all involved except the original writer or the writer that preceded you, and you rewrite the script. If you do a good enough job, you get to write the next rewrite. Or if they think you've done as much as you can, they hire another writer.

One page one rewrite I did, I was the sixth writer hired to work on the script. My version of the script ended up, with some minor changes, to be the shooting script when the film was made. I've also been writer number three out of five hired on another project. And the first writer hired out of four on another.

Producers want what they want and will hire as many writers as it takes to get the script to a point where they're satisfied. It's an everyday occurrence.

Like I said, you have four to six weeks, sometimes less, to accomplish this. It takes a lot of work, creativity, skill, and putting your butt into the seat for a lot of hours.

If I'm going to keep the structure of the story semi-close to the same as the original or last rewrite, I'll use the script I was sent as a template. If it's going to be a radical change, I'll start from a blank page with the original next to me for reference.

I've done up to four paid rewrites on the same project, getting notes from numerous people on the project every time. It's what professional screenwriters do to make a living. If you do it well, you get hired again and again.

There are many other types of rewrites you can get hired for besides the "page one" rewrite.

You can be hired to only fix the dialogue, doing what's called a "dialogue pass" on the script. I've done those.

You can get hired to do a "character pass" on the script, giving the characters more emotional layers and depth.

You can be hired to polish the script, not change it, but go through scene by scene, working on the "in late, out early" aspects of all the scenes, cleaning up unnecessary or convoluted action or dialogue, simplifying it. Seeing if there's a scene missing that will move the story more clearly.

You can be hired to take money out of the script for budgetary reasons, not changing the story at all, just what it would cost to make it. I get that one quite a bit.

You can get hired to write one scene they think they need.

You can get hired to add more humor, more story driven jokes to the script if it's a comedy or has comedy aspects.

You can get hired to radically change the lead character to fit a specific actor/actress and not change the basic story, and to handle the "ripple effects" of that kind of change to the story.

There are some writers who specialize in some of these particular jobs. There are other writers who can do many of them well. Producers know, over time, who does what and hires the writer who can most give them what they want. A lot of producers go back to the same writers time after time. Writers who have proved themselves. You want to be one of those writers.

You always have to keep in mind on any of these jobs, it's always what the producers or director want. You get to be very creative within that construct, but it's their money, therefore their way. That always has to be in the forefront of your mind as you do these jobs.

Each of these jobs is unique. To say there's one single way to approach them would be a disservice to you. Each story has its own life. Its own feel. Creatively, you approach each differently, using your experience to guide you. You get that experience writing your own specs, then being open to anything in rewriting them. Looking at them like you'd look at one of these rewrite jobs. That nothing in them can't be changed or improved. That's not easy for new writers who have a tendency to think their specs are mostly perfect. If you want to do this for a living you have to jettison that attitude right now.

The more you write, the more you work on your own craft, the more of these specific jobs you know how to do, the more valuable you become to producers and directors for these kinds of jobs.

ADAPTING A BOOK

Ok, they give you a 350-page novel and want you to write a 110-page script from it. How can you possibly tell the same story in 110 pages of screenplay format?

You can't.

In order to look like you've done that, you need to grab from that book the one true storyline in it. Determine the main plotline and major sub-plots of the story that need to be there and viciously cut everything else.

Me, I take a paper copy of the book and read it. I don't make any notes. I just read it. Then I wait a day or two and read it again with red and blue pens, using the red pen to cut what I think is unnecessary and the blue pen to make notes in the margins of the pages.

In most cases, everything not actively pushing the main storyline forward or not essential to major sub-plots has to go. Develop your outline or bullet points accordingly.

If the novel is written in third person. You still need to see whose point of view the novel is written from and start thinking of what you'll need to do to change that point of view to the audience's. Books can have all kinds of points of view. Films have one. The audience.

You look at that story and see how you can adapt it so it not only appeals to the fans of that book, but to people who have never read it, too. It's complex process that requires a lot of thought and skill.

What about if the book is written in first person? The temptation is to use voiceovers. That's the easier solution for a lot of writers who haven't done many adaptations. This should be resisted. Voiceovers can have their place, but audiences go to "see" films, not listen to them. Still, you need to take that first person story and transform it to the audience's point of view. This might entail inventing new characters and situations based on incidents in the book that are crucial to the story that can't be seen or heard any other way. It's complicated and a lot of work.

When I read a book the second time, I'm looking for what can be seen and heard on a screen. No thoughts. No intentions. It's all about action and dialogue. Nothing else. So, when you red-mark your book, circle the thoughts and intentions you need to change to action or dialogue, but remember, dialogue can be a trap. You have to avoid overt exposition at all costs. Again, subtext is your friend.

So, I, unlike my original specs, do write a complete bullet point step by step list of all the scenes in the film based on the book's story, so I have every plot point on one list. I also keep the book right next to me for reference. This is important.

So is whitespace on the page. Look at book adapted scripts. Read some of your favorite film scripts taken from novels. Look what they did and how they did it. Look what they didn't do that the novelist got to do.

You'll be tempted to keep some of the specifics you usually don't keep in screenplays, things that the author wrote like describing the clothing or the settings. This should also be resisted. Your job is to adapt the story alone.

Breaking the basic story down to its essence is crucial to success. Then you build it back up with characterization and action for the screen.

You may have to combine characters, change the order of some of the scenes, cut characters, jettison all kinds of what you think is wonderful stuff if it doesn't work for a film version.

This is not, however, a page one rewrite where you get to mess with the essence of the original story unless you've been told to by the people paying you to do this. The truer to the book you can be, the happier the fans are going to be. But don't let that keep you from writing scenes that weren't in the book to move the story forward the only way you can or combining scenes to do this.

There is no list or step by step way to guide a writer through this, again, because every book is different and requires different interpretations of the author's original story.

This is specialty writing. You can practice doing this by adapting a book you like that's in public domain, meaning the copyright has lapsed 70 years after the author's death. This is easily checked online and great practice. And at the end of it, you have a script you can show and maybe even option or sell.

Adapting a copyrighted book you have not optioned or purchased the rights to is, in my opinion, a complete and total waste of time. You can't show it to anyone or try and sell it. It belongs to either the author, their publishing company, or if it's a popular book, the rights have already probably been sold.

This doesn't mean you can't try and purchase or option the rights to a book you like if you want to. You'll find it very costly with no guarantees of a sale after you write it.

WRITE FOR HIRE

Here's the Holy Grail of jobs for writers. Where a studio, production company, or producer hire you to write a script for them. This can be as small as a cable movie for a minor network based on a story by the producer all the way up to the latest studio superhero sequel and everything in between.

It's a job where you're given the story, or a roadmap to the story, and paid to go write it. This is writing for hire. This is what you work for as a screenwriter.

I said earlier in the book that the writers up for these jobs all got into a position to compete for them by having success in independent film first. Films that got made from their scripts that were critical or financial successes in the low budget realm.

You need to know about this kind of job, but as far as me going over how to handle them? By the time you get one of these, you'll know what you're doing.

Have I had write for hire jobs? Yes, I have. A few. Nothing on the studio level yet, but I remain hopeful. They are not easy jobs to get.

CHAPTER 18

THE ACTING SCREENWRITER

I have been asked in the past, do you think you're a better screenwriter because of your acting experience?

I've spent many more years as an actor, or trying to be an actor, than I have as a screenwriter. In fact, I'm now over 25+ years as a member of the Screen Actors Guild and AFTRA. I've taken a slew of acting and improv classes in my life. I've taught acting classes in the past. I still find myself in front of a camera more than a couple of times a year on average.

I feel I'm qualified to talk about this.

So, how much has my acting experience helped me as a writer?

A whole lot. Maybe more than a whole lot.

Has it helped me write better dialogue? You bet. You still have to maintain the character you're trying to write. It just makes it easier to put the right words together in the right order if you look at it from an actor's, who will be playing your character, standpoint.

No actor wants wooden dialogue or dialogue that no human would say, which unfortunately is the dialogue in most new writers' scripts.

I see it all the time. Dialogue so unreal it's like space aliens wrote it. I've auditioned in the past for independent films where I got the "sides", which are actor's audition lines, and I've cringed at having to say what was on the page. Sometimes you just can't. There's no way to make it come out right because of the way it's written. How then, you ask, did such bad dialogue get as far as an audition? Beats the heck out of me. Tell me you haven't seen films with dialogue like this.

You just don't want to be the one who writes it.

Actors love great words. It makes them happy. When I was on the set of the film Jeff Willis and I wrote, *The Right Girl,* it made my year when all three leads told me, unprompted in completely separate conversations, that they loved the dialogue. They didn't have to do that. They could have just ignored me, but they didn't. Good writing means a lot to actors.

I'm bombarded a lot with questions and am asked for advice from actors all the time how I made the transition from actor to writer. I tell them all the same thing. It wasn't easy, but I think it was easier because I was an actor.

Acting experience has also helped me with constructing characters in my scripts. Giving characters more of what I think good actors might look for in the writing to help them understand who those characters are and more importantly, spurring them to want to play that part. I don't change story for what an actor might like, I think it helps me build more life into my characters that an actor can relate to.

What's this all about, Bob? So, acting helped you. How does that help a non-actor write?

Take some acting classes. Experience that side of it yourself. I'm not saying go out and try to make acting a career, but to see scripts from an actor's point of view. It can't help but make you a better screenwriter.

I've always thought that writers should take acting and improv classes. I've encouraged my writing friends to do it on more than one occasion. There are all kinds of acting classes everywhere. In LA you can't walk (sorry, it's LA, I mean drive) by a strip mall without seeing someplace that has acting classes. Community theaters all over the country have them. Look them up. Enroll in some. Experience it. Invest in your business.

In those classes you'll get scripts that aren't yours and have to tear apart the dialogue for their meaning, their subtext, then have to say those lines in ways to bring out that meaning. To understand when there's too much dialogue. To see how you can communicate with a look rather than words and be able to use that in your own scripts to make them more real.

It's not going to be easy, because acting isn't easy. But in its own way it takes the same kind of concentration that good writing takes. That, can do nothing but help you.

Or if acting intimidates you or you love it so much you want more, take improv classes. Those can help you come up with dialogue on the fly. I can't tell you all the times I've written zingy dialogue as fast as my fingers could type because of the improv training. Two characters going back and forth, the words coming to them as fast as it comes from me. No pre-planning except what I have to accomplish in the scene.

It's like an improv show on the page. In those shows, you're given parameters shouted from the audience, a lot of times very specific, and have to construct a scene on the spot. You do the same thing on the page with your scene parameters.

Theaters that do improv shows at night often have classes when they aren't doing the shows, taught by those same performers.

I've worked with actors who devote themselves to learning everything they can about their characters to get them right. To do them justice. I've watched and learned from them as they searched out even the littlest thing in the script to help them with backstory to bring a little more reality to their character. I've put those things into action myself as an actor. You don't think this has helped me writing scripts? To know what I need to write to give the characters that extra level of singularity that attracts good actors? Think again.

Everything you invest in, that you go out and do to educate yourself as a writer helps you as you go back and construct your scripts. Everyone is looking for an edge, but looking doesn't get you there. Doing gets you there. That one thing more that can take you to another level.

Participating in acting and improv classes and taking them seriously is one of those things. You may well stink at it. Lots of people do. Acting, or acting well, is a very hard thing to do. Acting in front of a camera with a hundred people standing around waiting for lunch is even harder. But I don't know a writer who wouldn't grow from that experience. Gain insight. It's one more building block in your career.

And who knows, maybe someday you'll beat me out for a part or I'll be acting in some film you wrote. It's all there for you to have. It's up to you as a screenwriter to find every advantage you can over those writers who don't want to do the hard work and don't understand there's more to it than sitting down and writing.

CHAPTER 19

GRAB BAG

This section was suggested to me by a friend: that I have a chapter to cover some of the most asked questions I get that weren't covered in the other chapters.

"How do I pitch my original spec to producers?"

Pitch, as in "Sales Pitch". Which is exactly what this is. I can go back to the car analogy. You're kicking the tires of your script. Selling them the sizzle, hoping they'll buy the steak. Ok, that was a mixed analogy, but you get it.

A pitch is your spoken query letter. You can have anywhere from five to fifteen minutes to do this in a meeting. The meeting may go a lot longer, but that all depends on how you handle this part of it. Getting their attention and getting them interested enough in your story to prolong the meeting.

How do you do this in such a short time? You practice, but beyond that it's what you practice.

You don't have time to tell them the whole story, so don't try. What you want them to spike to is your premise, your protagonist's journey, who they are and what they'll face. You don't have to give them the ending. You don't have to reveal twists.

Your real goal is to get them emotionally involved with the pitch.

When I pitched Extracurricular Activities, I got them involved like this…

"Remember that kid at your high school? The one who wore polo shirts and khakis and set the curve in all your classes? The one who got along much better with the teachers than any of the other kids? The one your parents told you that you needed to be like? What if he also had an afterschool job killing parents for the kids at his school?"

Then, I hit them with my logline, my film comparison, if I have a good one, move to most specifics and pause occasionally to wait for questions or comments. You need to give them time for those.

This worked a lot more than it didn't. I used their memories to start. They had a face from their past to attach to my story immediately. Maybe their own face. Doesn't matter.

You stir up any kind of emotion you can to get them actively thinking about your project. To get them thinking, "Hmmm, I could do something with this."

You want to get them to understand your unique take on a genre. You emphasize what makes your horror or romantic comedy different enough to make them want to do something with it.

Making them understand they have an opportunity to have a project that's unique is a lot better than reciting a bunch of bullet points from the story.

You don't get emotional. You leave that to them. You don't talk about how the script affects you. The pitch is never about you. It's about them and your script or series. Leave yourself out of it. That just wastes time and bores them. They don't care about you.

Putting together a spoken pitch is hard work if you want to do it right. Practice it with everyone you know. Ask them what questions they have. Hone it. Change it. Ask them if they'd buy it if they had the money.

And ask for the truth.

I take pitches very seriously. I put in as much work on them as I do writing a script. That script depends on me being able to pitch it to the best of my ability.

"What kinds of meetings will I get to go to as a screenwriter?"

MEETINGS

There are basically four types. There can be combinations of any of these.

GENERAL MEETINGS

This is what's called The Water Bottle Tour. You go into a production company for a meeting based on your rep being able to set it up so producers and production companies can see you, meet you, size you up, and have you give them an overview of what you do and have them give you an overview of what they're looking for.

It is a grand dance. There is no specific project they are dealing with. You talk about your successes. You pitch them some of your scripts that might be a fit for them.

Of course, you did your homework before you went. You learned every little thing about them you could, so don't pitch the wrong kinds of things because that's not smart.

These meetings can last fifteen minutes, not good, to an hour if they're really good.

You go in relaxed because you have nothing to lose, because you're going in there with nothing. At the best of these meetings, they'll ask for you to send a script or two to them, or they send you a script to look at for a rewrite job. At the worst of them, they rush you out with an emergency phone call they have arranged to take after 15 minutes, if they need an escape.

These kinds of meetings can lead to great things, but mostly lead to nothing to begin with. As you leave the three people waiting in the lobby are there for the same general meeting.

Remember what I said about desperation? This is where you really can't show it. Those are the 15-minute meetings. You don't hog the conversation. You listen. You ask intelligent questions. You answer theirs honestly. And maybe, you get asked back for a formal…

PITCH MEETING

This meeting is where you sit around a conference table or in an executive's office to make that formal pitch we talked about earlier for one of your projects.

You have about an average of 5 to 10 minutes for a movie and maybe 20 for a series to pitch your film or show. Sometimes less if they pass before you're done. These meetings can last an hour or more if they're interested or they can get another emergency call and you're gone in five minutes.

You have longer for each pitch if they start asking you questions, which is very good. Before you go into the meeting, anticipate as many of these questions as you can, so you're ready for them. But, trust me on this, you always get a couple you couldn't have anticipated. Have those answers, too.

Hint: Never ever lie about anything. They always find out. If you don't know the answer to a question, "I don't know, but I'll find out" is a perfectly satisfactory answer. They'll appreciate you didn't feed them a bunch of bull, if you didn't know the answer.

You practice your pitch for these meetings. You have it down cold. These aren't meetings you just "wing". Your knowledge about every aspect of your project has to be on the tip of your tongue.

These meetings can be life changing. Treat them that way. With the respect they deserve. Don't interrupt people. Don't argue with people. Listen and understand what they say. If you don't understand something, say "I'm not clear exactly what you mean". They'll explain themselves.

Be flexible. If they give you a good idea, tell them "Wow, what a great idea. Thank you." They may have never heard that from a writer before.

If you think I'm kidding; I was in a big conference room at a cable network in a production meeting on the rewrite of a script for a film going into production. About 8 to 10 people were sitting around a big table, all eyes on me to solve the story and character problems for this script I was hired to rewrite.

They had a long list of problems and I was coming up with answers to solve them, with others throwing out ideas, too. One big network exec suggested something for a particular sticky problem. It was a great idea. It not only helped that problem, but may have solved three or four down the line, too.

I looked at her and said, "Wow. That's a terrific idea. You just made the script about 60% better." She looked shocked. I smiled and said, "You ok?"

She grinned and said, "I've never had a writer say that to me. That the note was great." I thought, "Really?" I can't believe there are writers who wouldn't say that for an idea or note that could make them look better with their name on the screen as writer? To be appreciative?

So now, if I get great notes, and you do get them, I make it a point to tell whoever gave it to me how good it is and how much I appreciate it. It's about respect and being a team player.

Even if your pitch fails and you get a pass, you thank them for the opportunity to be there. There are hundreds, if not thousands, of writers who would love to be in your shoes just for the chance to pitch their projects in a meeting like that. You are one of a small percentage who get into that room, rejection or not. And if you comport yourself with graciousness and respect, you'll get back in there as soon as you have another idea they might be interested in.

Businesslike.

OWA PITCH MEETING

Open Writing Assignments are sometimes offered directly to writers they know will do a great job because the project is their particular wheelhouse. It's theirs if they want it. I've been offered rewrite jobs without having to compete for them. It's a very nice thing.

But when they don't have someone in mind? Or they want to see what's out there? They'll find six to ten writers, maybe more, to compete for the job. Those writers don't know who they're competing with most of the time, but that's the way producers do it.

If you're one of those writers, you'll be given the script they want to rewrite or the story or the book to adapt. Then you do a whole bunch of hard work to put together your presentation on how you would approach the job. Then you go back later and pitch, yes, sales pitch. A pitch you have practiced extensively. They listen, ask questions, you hope they don't take an emergency call, and are impressed with your take on the project, or not. They never say in the room.

Remember, it's never about you. It's about the project, whatever it is.

Then you leave and the next writer comes in. All you can do is choose a specific approach and stick with it. If you're all over the place, that's worse. Be uber-prepared and hope that your approach is the one they were looking for.

I get my share of these jobs, but I also get rejected for them. It's part of being this kind of writer.

You don't wait by the phone to hear. You go on with your life. If you get it? Great. If not? Just another day on the job. They don't call unless you get it.

AGENT / MANAGER MEETINGS

These are the kinds of meetings you only get if the reps are truly interested in repping you. They've read your scripts. They've looked up your social media history. Oh yes, they look at that. Just a word of warning.

They want to see how you are under pressure. How you'll be in a room. They may ask you to pitch to them. They'll ask you who you know in the industry and what those people might say about you. And then, later, they'll call them. So, don't lie.

This is also your chance to ask them about how they operate their business. You have the right to ask them anything, within reason.

You can ask managers about whether they're also producers. You can ask how they plan to get your work out. You can ask if they have to approve everything you write. You can ask about their success stories. And if you don't like their answers you can say no, too.

They get to ask you about your success stories. Again, don't lie. They always find out the truth.

Don't sign any contract until you've had a chance to look it over with a lawyer or a contract expert. If there's something you don't like, ask about it.

This is a business relationship. You don't work for an agent or manager. This is very important. You should be on equal footing. You have a right to know everything about your business. The agent or manager has a right to ask you anything and if they rep you, expect you to follow through on anything they set up for you.

I get asked all the time, "If I sell something on my own without my manager or get a write for hire job they didn't put me up for, do I have to pay my manager?"

My feeling about this? Yes. Absolutely. You want an honest and above-board relationship. You want that manager or agent to trust you as much as you trust them. Plus, they're more adept at dealing with any contract problems that arise and if you haven't paid them, how can you ask for help? Always pay your reps.

Again, be businesslike, without fear or desperation. If you get a meeting like this, it puts you in a small percentage of writers trying to do this. Treat it that way.

One other thing about agents and managers, if you get one, the fastest way to lose one is to bug them. Once a week to check in, fine, but no more. They will call you if they need something from you or have a meeting or a deal.

If you're in the middle of a deal, option or sale, negotiations on a contract, yes, you'll talk more. But these people have other clients, other responsibilities. You aren't the only one. They also have their own lives. If you have a reason to call, call. If not, fight the urge. Once a week is enough, or once every two weeks. They will appreciate the way you handle your business and be more responsive.

"I hear about NDAs. What exactly are they?"

An NDA is a Non-Disclosure Agreement. If you get a job writing a superhero movie, they will make you sign one of these. It says you will not disclose anything you are doing or anything about the project you are working on to anyone outside of that project. Producers and production companies have writers who are doing OWAs sign these documents all the time. There are some serious repercussions for breaking one of these NDAs. It's not pretty.

The people who have you sign these do not do this casually. They enforce them. You sign one. You do what it says.

Ok Bob, what about the NDA a producer sends me when they want to read my script? Sometimes, a producer will ask you to sign an agreement in order to send them a script.

I do know what those are. It's a release of responsibility agreement, not an NDA. Lots of new writers call these documents NDAs and they're not.

What these release of responsibility documents mean is if they read your script and they already have something like it, or find something like it down the road, you can't come back and sue them saying they stole your idea. Do I sign these when asked? I do. Why? I want them to read my script. Do I think they'll steal it? No. Why? Because it's easier to buy it and less costly.

Read these agreements, make up your own mind. If they have something objectionable in them, ask about it. Find out what they mean. Then either sign and send or don't sign and don't send. But these documents are not NDAs.

Ok Bob, I heard about writers making producers sign NDAs before letting them read their scripts. Is that ok?

Think about this. You want a producer to show your script to others in the industry. Other producers. Finance people. Actors. Directors. And you're going to send them a document to sign stipulating they can't show it to anyone? That's what an NDA is. The first two words are non-disclosure, Really? You think this is a good idea?

Doing this kind of paranoid amateur move, sending a producer an NDA to sign before sending a script they requested? It's an instant rejection before even reading your script of both your script and you. You're done with them. And they remember.

Don't do this. It's a horrible mistake to make. You can't recover from it.

"Can I write my script with a specific actor in mind?"

Can you? Sure. Should you? In my opinion, no. Writing for a specific actor or actress, making your protagonist speak in this actor's voice or cadence? Describing the character that way? Basing their personality on that actor or actress, hoping that they'll do your film before there's money, a producer, or a director?

I once read a script where the protagonist was actually described as "a Denzel Washington type or actually Denzel, I hope".

What happens to your script if Denzel says no? Which the chances are very strong, like 99.9%, he'd do. What happens to any script tailored to any particular actor or actress when they say, "Not interested"? It means you have a script that's not going to get a lot of attention from other actors or actresses.

It means yet another rewrite that you might not have needed if you'd just written the characters to fit the story, rather than shoehorning an actor's personality into it.

If you have a star who has attached to your project for any reason, then yes, you might have to tailor the script for them. If not? You write your characters to be the best they can be in the story you're trying to tell. You want to write characters that actors want to play, not the other way around.

I know some writers like to picture actors as the characters as they write, but I think that's very limiting. You might have that character do something better if you hadn't been picturing a particular actor.

In *Extracurricular Activities*, I wrote characters that, to me, had their own lives. No thought of actors at all. They were living the story as those people. One of the characters was the town police chief. To me, a tough, no nonsense chief that stood up to Cliff, a detective who was one of the leads. I wrote the chief as a man.

The casting director, reading the script, saw something else in that chief and they cast Charmin Lee, an amazing African American actress, who was so good in the part I was thrilled and told her that maybe too many times.

And because I wrote the part for the character instead of any actor, the dialogue barely had to be changed for Charmin. She nailed it as the character I wrote.

Unless I've been told to write a part because an actor has been cast, I never do it. It has served me well, as actor after actor on sets has thanked me for writing such a fun character for them to play. I wish I could bottle it.

It reinforces that I need to keep writing my characters for the story and not for actors. You should do that, too. You'll write deeper richer characters.

"Do I have any say in who gets cast in my film?"

As I said in an earlier chapter, the writer has zero, as in no, say in which actors get cast as the characters they've written. They might ask you who you want to see in it, but mostly they don't ask or care.

They see the actors they want as they read it. They make their decisions based on their ideas, not yours. They're also paying for it.

Get it out of your head right now that you will have the actors you want in your film. If they ask you who you'd like, tell them. Get it out of your system, then be a cheerleader as they cast amazing people you never thought of because they really do know better than you who to cast. With one exception, in one of my films, I have been overwhelmingly supportive of the casting choices on my projects and am often surprised by the choices in a very good way.

There's a reason that producers hire casting agents. They've got the contacts. They know the acting agents. They know actors you could never think of.

Professional casting agents are amazing at what they do. It's their job to find the perfect potential choices for the director and producers to choose from for each role. I've watched in awe as they do their job.

Again, don't ask in your contracts for casting approval. You'll never get it and it's a really amateur thing to do. Let the people who do it for a living handle it. Those casting agents will never ask if they can rewrite your script. They know it's your job. Let them do theirs.

"How do you find a writing partner?"

I've read on screenwriting boards, all over the internet, posts where writers are asking, "Who wants to write a script with me? I have a great idea and thought it would be cool to partner with someone."

There's nothing wrong with writing with a partner. I've written four scripts with a couple of different partners and both experiences made me a better writer and I got a couple of lifelong friends out of it. Plus, one produced film so far.

But I didn't post on the internet looking for them. Finding a stranger to team up with is a recipe for disaster. You know nothing about them, how they write, what their work ethic is, or more importantly, if they're crazy or not.

If you feel you'd like to work with another writer on a project, take your time. Have it be a writer you know or are familiar with, even if it's on screenwriting boards you frequent. Read their work. Let them read yours. Look at both styles. Will they mesh or clash?

Talk to them about writing philosophies. Agree on a plan. How you will structure the write? Who will do what and when? Have an agreement on partnership splits.

Most importantly, have a written contract with each other. Make the script both of your priorities until it's finished. There's nothing worse than the half-finished script with a partner. They never seem to get completed. If only one of the writers finishes it, you can bet the other will be claiming their ownership. Then it becomes adversarial. That's exactly what you don't want.

Be careful. You also want the other writer to be as careful as you are. You want them to ask you as much as you ask them. This is a marriage. A permanent one on anything you write together. Make sure you get along outside of the writing aspect of your relationship.

If you go by my experience? It works like a charm if you have the right partner. I'd write with both of these writers again in a minute. But I knew them before we wrote a word.

That's the person you need to take the time and look for if this is what you want to do.

Picking some random person who says, "Yeah, let's do it" without doing your due diligence will always be a resounding failure.

Writing any good script is a ton of hard work. Why embark on that journey with someone you know nothing about? Again, desperate writers do really rash and stupid stuff. Be smart and, again, treat it like a business partnership, and you'll have a much better chance at ending up with something you're proud of. And a new or better friend.

"Will I get to be on the set of my film?"

Maybe. Times are changing in that more and more writers are allowed on sets these days.

What do you mean allowed? Isn't it my story?

Your job is done when they go into production. On occasion, some writers are on set to work, but only with the director, or if it's an A-list actor, maybe that actor. You'll know when you're supposed to do this because they hire you to do it.

Film is a director's medium. On the set, they're the ultimate boss. This is something you have to learn, know, and respect.

They decide if you can come on the set, along with the producers. It's a gift. It's an honor. They do it sometimes to reward a writer who has done their job well, been cooperative, and not caused any problems or asked for too much.

If you get to go to a set for a visit, or are allowed to come and go as you please, and I've had it both ways, you have to understand your role.

Your role is to watch everything and enjoy it to pieces. If the director asks you for your opinion on something, you answer.

You cannot under any circumstances:

1. Make suggestions about or question anything you see. I mean…anything
2. Talk to the actors about their characters unless the director tells you to.
3. Make suggestions about or question anything. It's here twice because I'm not kidding.

If you do any of these things. They will ask you to leave and never come back. And good luck being invited to the premiere. It's the number one no-no for any writer.

But if you're there just to watch, Here's my advice.

Find a quiet place to watch them shoot your scenes. Watch carefully as your characters come to life in front of your eyes, saying what you told them to. Watch as the scene unfolds. Be amazed as actors take your dialogue and do things you never thought about with it, bringing to it more life than you could have ever imagined.

Then, quietly wipe that tear from your eye, because you will have one. You'll have a few. Then go enjoy the food.

As a screenwriter, I cannot tell you how personally satisfying it is to watch this happening in front of you. It makes all the rejections and disappointments of the past fade away.

You can talk to the crew. You can joke with the actors, if they're not preparing to work. You can talk to the producer about how it's going. You can talk to the director.

You can't suggest or question anything. Just making sure you know.

"What about working other jobs on sets? Will this help me as a writer?"

You bet it will. It helped me. I think every writer who wants to do this should spent some time on sets to see how making a film actually works.

I got an education as a film extra that I use every day as I write. I was an extra on multiple films, trying to break in as an actor, some 100 million-dollar films actually. It was eye opening.

One day, I got booked as an extra on the very first day of shooting on the TV series *Nash Bridges,* as a uniformed cop, back in that wheelhouse. Only one of two extras that night. So, like an idiot, I sidled up to where Don Johnson was and engaged him in conversation, made him laugh a couple of times, and was never used as an extra that night. Later on, the set 2nd AD came up to me and said he saw me with Don. He read me the riot act for talking to him, saying I'd never work on the show again because extras aren't supposed to talk to the stars, which I knew, but c'mon we were the only two people out there at the time. I felt terrible. Once again, I flaunted the "rules".

Next thing I know, I get a call from extras casting saying that the *Nash* people asked for me specifically and wanted me back to be in the *Nash Bridges* police station as a cop extra. I won't bore you with the details of everything, but I ended up doing 122 episodes of the show as that same character. Even got a name (Carl Hoskins) and a promotion (to Sergeant), in season 1 episode 8. Did a few episodes over those years in that character as a principal actor, but was a glorified extra the rest of the time. Sometimes not even glorified.

Those six seasons gave me an opportunity I could never have gotten in any regular film school. About halfway through the first season I went to Don and asked him if, when I was there working, I could have free run of the set to learn about every department. Exactly what everyone on the crew did and how and why they did it. I got a big smile and pat on the shoulder and he said, "How do you think I learned? You have my blessing." I did it every season for six seasons. Not only has it helped me immensely as a writer, but it led to some meaningful lifelong friendships.

I learned about electric, lighting, the camera department, (even got to put on the steady-cam), props, set dressing, effects, sound (thank you Aggie), stunts, unit production, you name it, I asked them about it and sucked up untold amounts of priceless knowledge. I watched the directors. I saw who was good, who was bad, and learned from it all. I found out where to put cameras, where not to put cameras, what lens to use where and why, about coverage, rules of thirds, lines of sight, you name it, I learned it. And everyone was great about it, too.

My understanding of what it takes to make a film and what things cost has helped me beyond words, again, as a writer. I can speak with knowledge in production meetings and not illicit rolled eyes. Truthfully, it has been a Godsend in working with directors and producers because I understand what it takes physically to make a film.

Now, a word about the man himself. Don Johnson. To me he was nothing but gracious, kind, and one of the smartest guys I have ever seen on a set. That man knows. He doesn't miss a thing. I owe him a debt. He paid me to go to film school while I was writing my first scripts. I was able to network with the people on that set which led to my first options and boatloads of great contacts I still use today. I wouldn't have the writing career I do without Don Johnson.

You can get on sets as an extra, too. They are the bottom of the film food chain, but if you pay attention, network the correct way, there is so much you can learn. And you'll make some pocket change.

Most states and big cities have extras casting companies that supply people for films that come there. There are online companies to register with. Most college film programs have a need for them. Search them out. Get yourself on a set. Soak it all in.

It is absolutely worth it.

"How did the reality of getting one of your scripts made differ from your expectations?"

Allow me to use the experience I had on the originals spec script Jeff Willis and I wrote, *The Right Girl*. A kind of romantic comedy where we defied expectations of the genre and had the two leads not get together at the end.

The original script was funny, different, had unexpected twists and turns and the final "What?" ending where the two leads go in different directions, as the female lead goes out on her own to learn more about her new self before committing to any relationship. It was real. It was an ending a lot of people who read the script loved.

The same company that made *Help for the Holidays* asked to read this script, after I pitched it to them and, to our surprise, optioned it.

Then over the next few months, Jeff and I did seven paid rewrites with multiple sets of production company notes and made huge changes, ok, monstrous changes, with even more notes coming from the network with even more changes and even more notes from production execs as it got closer to production, and then finally, the director notes.

To say the script was extremely different from the original script we wrote is way too mild. It still had our stamp on it, the humor, but the movie we wanted to see originally from our idea and the movie they wanted to see were night and day different. With, you already guessed it, a happy ending where they got together.

We had to please more than a dozen people we got notes from before the film was made. All who wanted to put their stamp on it somewhere, too. This is the development process I talked about earlier. They removed entire subplots and counted on us to add new ones in the direction they wanted it taken. They axed characters. Changed characters. What they did not do was change the overall premise. Yes, they added the happy ending, but kept the spine of the story to that ending intact.

When I asked them why they bought it, like I always do even if it's one of mine, they said it was that storyline, that premise which was fresh. So, we had that going for us. In the meantime, they kept throwing out our original scenes from the spec, and then gradually letting us put a lot of them back in as we went through all those rewrites. One of those full circle things that happens if you stay with your own project and don't get replaced. Another writer would never have gone back to our scenes.

That's why you cooperate, are a team player, and are easy to work with.

After it went into production, I was able to go to the set for a full day because the producers liked me. I also had a past connection to the director. I had worked with him many times before as he'd directed two of my other movies. I met him originally when he directed two episodes of *Nash Bridges* a lifetime ago. Made it easy to get a set visit. I still didn't have any suggestions or questions. I met the cast, who I was very happy with. Watched them shoot scenes and teared up a little.

There on set, I immediately fell in love with Anna Hutchison (*Cabin in the Woods, Spartacus*), who was playing our main character. She was our Kimberly. It was amazing and kind of an out of body experience to watch. I would use her again as an actor in a second. Add in Costas Mandylor, who I also knew from *Nash Bridges*. He pointed at me and said, "Hey, I know you." And Gail O'Grady, who was also there that day, and I was a happy camper at what I witnessed.

One of the producers gave me a tour of the other sets for the film on the soundstage. It was a good day.

I wish Jeff could have come with me, but he was in Brazil doing humanitarian work while I was hanging around the craft service table, showing me up once again. I'm not kidding. He was in Brazil building houses for the poor or something. An amazing man who puts his money and time where his mouth is.

As for expectations? I knew every word of that final script. Every word.

Then they sent us a director's cut. I couldn't wait to see it.

I popped it in my computer to watch, and once again it was a huge lesson. A lesson to writers everywhere.

It's never what you expect, even when you watch it being shot. Even when you wrote what you thought was the shooting script.

When you as a writer have your finished script, you see it in your head, or should. You see the scenes play out. You hear the line interpretations the way you want to hear them. But you're not the director, unless you are, then ignore me, nor are you the actors, who bring their own skills with them. Skills, if they're good actors, you can't fathom until you see what they do with your dialogue and action. Things you never thought of. There were times in the film as I watched where I was stunned at how wonderfully the lines were interpreted and how differently than I had heard them in my head.

The direction was solid, but then I expected that. Some great camera use that really moved the story well. Zero problems with the way it was shot. Great sets, costumes, and production design. The edit was good too. A little long, but it was a director's cut.

But since these are your characters and you know them inside and out, you sit and pray for them to be what you envisioned. Good actors bring their own life to your characters you can't anticipate. Again, Anna was a revelation in the cut. The character of Kimberly, as we wrote her, is a very vain and arrogant and funny, we hoped, person at the start of the film. We knew the actor playing her would have to be able to skate a thin line, not make her so unlikeable that the audience didn't care about her journey. Anna did it with a classy ease that brought layers of dimension and humor we couldn't have dreamed about. She was what I had pictured Kimberly to be and much more.

But then, a lot of the time, what you picture doesn't happen. Costas' interpretation of his character was nothing like we'd pictured. Where our written character was lighter and more comic relief, Costas brought a serious twinge to him. Gravitas that we didn't expect or write, honestly, in the character. Don't get me wrong, I liked it. A lot. It was terrific. I never saw it in the character. He did.

And Gail O'Grady was more sophisticated and urbane than we wrote her character and it worked too. Dorian Harewood brought his considerable skills to his character, playing him exactly the way we imagined. Overall, the acting in it was first class and I thank these pros from the bottom of my heart.

A lot of the scenes were word for word what we wrote and I can't tell you how exciting that is. You'd have to experience it to understand.

Sometimes you get really lucky and sometimes you scratch your head, at the same film.

There's a whole big scene neither one of us wrote in the middle of the film. Smack in the middle. A scene that wasn't in our final draft or even discussed with us, ever. It wasn't awful. It just didn't add anything to the story. It's there and I have no idea where it came from or why it's there, one of those surprises you have to expect as a writer. And the choice of the producers and/or the director, because in the end it is their choice and not yours.

And the last scene is completely different from what we wrote, too. Not a bad ending scene at all, I like it ok, just not close to what we wrote. A different direction yet again. A new ending that they rewrote while making the film, I think. Something that happens every day, by the way. As a writer you have to shrug it off and understand because, again, it's not your decision to make.

Jeff called me after he watched it and we talked for quite a while. Were we happy with the film? You bet. Very happy. Our names are in the titles in big letters, right before the director's. You can't beat that.

Is it our script the way we pictured it? Well, no.

It never is.

In this case, I'm happy to say I think it is just as good and in some places better. That's not always the case. You need to understand that, too.

I have another film I wrote I think is unwatchable because of what they did to it in production. It's as far from the script I was paid for and turned in as any film ever.

You have to throw out your expectations in this business and only live in the reality of it.

And finally…

"How do you get over Writer's Block?"

You write your way out of it. Don't mope. Don't cry. Don't do anything but put your butt in a chair and write your way out of it.

This is the only thing that works.

CHAPTER 20

END CREDITS

CREDITS

Time to talk about your name on the screen. It's kind of a life changing thing to see.

I talked about putting in your non-union contract that you get screen credit that says: Written by, or Screenplay by. You absolutely can ask for that, especially if you've compromised on pay, and even if you haven't.

Can you not get credited on your own project? Rarely, but you can get, if you don't protect yourself contractually, Story by: credit and not Screenplay by: credit.

How does this happen? When there's nothing left of your original script and they credit the writer or writers who rewrote everything, under instruction from producers and/or the director.

Will you ever have to share credit on your own project? Absolutely, if that writer has changed a significant amount, or all of your script, and you have writing credit written into your contract. It looks like this…

SCREENPLAY BY

You and That Other Writer

This is the difference between "&" and "and" in the titles. When you see:

SCREENPLAY BY

You & That Other Writer

This means you and that other writer were partners on the original script. If you replace the "&" with "and", it tells everyone that it was rewritten by the other writer. Now when you see films with titles like this…

SCREENPLAY BY

You & That Other Writer

And Yet Another Writer

You'll know who partners were and who was hired.

No one is going to be your advocate better than you. If it's non-union ask for the credit to be in the contract.

What about the WGA? Are they better?

WGA projects have their credits determined by the Guild. The original writer almost always gets some kind of credit, but not always.
The best way to protect yourself is to stay with the project as long as you can. That means being cooperative, changing the things they want in the script, not getting angry about it, and getting it finished by any deadline you have.

Sometimes, though, even if you do all these things, they still bring in another writer for a fresh take and fresh ideas.

For credits? Dream about an individual credit, be happy with a shared one.

CHAPTER 21

WELL, DO YOU STILL WANT TO BE A SCREENWRITER?

Good.

Every time I do an interview anywhere, I get asked if I only had one piece of advice for screenwriters, what would it be? Answer is always the same.

"Don't give up!"

That's it.

You'll face all those things I wrote about in this book. Not a lot of them are pretty. Some are depressing. You'll face rejection. And setbacks. And near misses. And frustration.

But when you have that first read request from a query.

That first option deal.

Your first sale.

Your first Greenlight.

Your first production meeting.

When you get an Agent or Manager.

Your first Open Writing Assignment.

Your first set visit.

Go to your first premiere.

See your name on any screen in the credits?

It's ALL worth it. All the pain and time and sweat and work.

You can do this. I did it. That means anyone can.

THANK YOU

I want to thank my wife, Margie, for putting up with me not giving up for all those hard years trying to do this. She's a saint. My best friend and best critic. Plus, she finds most of my typos. Love you.

My kids, Natalie, David, and Stephanie, who also put up with my quest for years. They know this is all I ever wanted to do and supported me all the way. I love you.

Jeff Willis for being my good and great friend and partner in crime.

My real-life writer friends. I love you all.

Jay Lowi. I love you, man. You make dreams come true.

Don Johnson. No you. No career. Deep thanks.

Kathy Ide for your invaluable book advice.

Pea Woodruff and Jim Kalergis, for being my ears and eyes.

Bill Hall for the book title.

Jamie Lee Scott for the cover and walking me through publication.

Film Twitter. You all are nuts, but my kind of nuts.

The Screenwriters who all want this as much as I did, that make up the membership of the Facebook Screenwriting Board. It's an insane asylum, but it's my insane asylum.

To the producers I've worked with, thank you for believing in what I do and can bring to any project. I appreciate everything you do to get miracles made.

To producers everywhere; the book is done, I'm available again.

I hope you got something you can use out of this book. If you got one thing, I'm happy.

When I first started this screenwriting quest, I was helped and supported by some of the most wonderful pros in the industry. They helped me get through doors. To meet people who could advance my career. They didn't have to. They did anyway. I cannot thank you enough.

If I can give a little of that back to you here, thank you for allowing me to do it.

Now get your ass in the seat and write.